TRUST
THE
GRIND

TRUST THE GRIND

HOW WORLD-CLASS ATHLETES GOT TO THE TOP

JEREMY BHANDARI

CORAL GABLES

For permission requests, please contact the publisher at:
Mango Publishing Group
2850 S Douglas Road, 2nd Floor
Coral Gables, FL 33134 USA
info@mango.bz

For special orders, quantity sales, course adoptions and corporate sales, please email the publisher at sales@mango.bz. For trade and wholesale sales, please contact Ingram Publisher Services at customer.service@ingramcontent.com or +1.800.509.4887.

Trust the Grind: How World-Class Athletes Got to the Top

Library of Congress Cataloging-in-Publication number: 2019954713
ISBN: (p) 978-1-64250-244-2 (e) 978-1-64250-245-9
BISAC category code: YAN051200, YOUNG ADULT NONFICTION / Social Topics / Self-Esteem & Self-Reliance

Printed in the United States of America

To my friend PJ, who passed away in 2018 at just twenty-two years old after a battle with osteosarcoma. In November 2016, PJ had his first surgery to remove a tumor in his hip. The following are two passages from PJ's post, "The depth of my gratitude is equal to the height of my success—and I feel victorious," which can be found on Boston Children's Hospital's pediatric health blog.

"When I was first going through treatment, I learned that sometimes you have to take it one day at a time, one hour at a time, or even one second at a time. Those hard times taught me to appreciate all the great moments I have in a day. We all have so many great moments that we take for granted. I learned that if I just took a second to change my mentality and perspective, I could enjoy everything so much more."

"They told me I'd never walk again, at least not without a really bad limp and a cane. But after four months of physical therapy, I was walking on a single cane. The next summer, I hiked to the top of Mt. Monadnock with two of my friends, Gaby and Greg. I just kept working at it and doing a little more every day until I could hike without crutches or a cane. I started doing hikes at Noanet Woodlands in Dover every day and decided I wanted to try Mt. Monadnock. That hike was way more than I expected, and I really had to push it to get to the top. But, once I was there, it felt like such an accomplishment. I had been told I wouldn't be able to walk, and there I was at the top of a mountain."

Thank you for epitomizing greatness as an athlete, student, friend, son, and brother. Your legacy will live on forever.

TABLE OF CONTENTS

INTRODUCTION

A Look into This Wonderful World

August 4, 1901. Louis Daniel Armstrong is born in New Orleans, Louisiana. Having a knack for music, Armstrong flourished as a trumpeter, composer, and vocalist. To this day, "Louie" is considered one of the most authoritative figures in jazz. Are you familiar with the song "What a Wonderful World"? You know, the one that starts out with:

> I see trees of green, red roses too
> I see them bloom for me and you
> And I think to myself what a wonderful world

The elegant voice behind the euphoric lyrics was Armstrong, who recorded the song in his sixties. By 2014, the single had been downloaded over two million times in the United States after it was released digitally. In 1999, twenty-eight years after Armstrong's death, the song made its way into the Grammy Hall of Fame.

August 4, 2019. On a day when we should be celebrating Armstrong's legacy and the "clouds of white" and "colors of the rainbow," that he so gracefully described in his music, we are forced to captivate some stomach-churning statistics. According to the Gun Violence Archive, there had been 255 reported mass shootings so far that year in the US. By the not-for-profit corporation's definition, a mass shooting is any incident in which four or more people are shot. 216 days into the year. 255 mass shootings.

According to the Anxiety and Depression Association of America, Major Depressive Disorder, a mental health disorder specified by frequently depressed mood or loss of enthusiasm in activities, affects more than sixteen million American adults. One in four children between the ages of thirteen and eighteen suffers from anxiety. As said in national survey data released by the Centers for Disease Control and Prevention (CDC), between 2011 and 2014, 11 percent of Americans, of all ages, reported taking at least one antidepressant medication in the past month. To put that in perspective, if you looked around a baseball diamond during a game, one of those nine individuals used antidepressants within the last thirty days. Just three decades ago, it was reported that less than one in fifty people (2 percent) did.

Stopbullying.gov reported that seven out of ten young people claimed to have witnessed bullying at school. Heck, even three out of every ten people admitted that they had bullied others. The 2017 School Crime Supplement (National Center for Education Statistics and Bureau of Justice) found that around 20 percent of students age twelve to eighteen experienced bullying in the past school year.

In 2017, CBS News published an article on happiness in the workplace. The article referenced a recent Gallup study, which reported that 51 percent of full-time employees in America are not engaged at work. Half of our working society is spending at least forty hours per week unsatisfied.

Yes, you could absolutely make the argument for gun laws in America. You could also come up with a pretty good case for why adults in the work force deserve more vacation. Creating a petition for change in the education system wouldn't be a bad idea either, especially since public schooling has been run the same way since well before the internet.

But what if I told you there was a way to continue to see the kindness and light in the world, even with all these sad truths? Before you call me crazy, read this Jack Canfield quote:

*"If you can tune into your purpose and really align with it,
setting goals so that your vision is an expression of that
purpose, then life flows much more easily."*

You see, when we have a sense of purpose, we give ourselves
a real reason to get up every single day. A sense of purpose
picks us up when life knocks us down. It can also help us create
the life that we aspire to live. A purpose forces us to focus on
self-growth, and spreading positivity and love to those around
us, rather than expressing anger and unrolling hatred out to
the world. By identifying a motive, we are able to appreciate
"babies crying" and seeing "friends shaking hands."

Remember when Benjamin Franklin said, "Our new
Constitution is now established and has an appearance that
promises permanency; but in this world, nothing can be said
to be certain, except death and taxes"? While many argue
about who coined the latter half of this quote, the premise is
understood by all. With so much uncertainty in the world, the
only guarantees in life are death and the fact that we will be
faced with tax payments for as long as we are breathing.

However, I can make an argument that everyone, and I mean
everyone, certainly seeks success and happiness. I mean, have
you ever met someone that wakes up each morning and plans
on being sad and a failure? Of course not. With that said, the
idiomatic expression should really be, "Nothing is certain in life
except death, taxes, and the pursuit of happiness and success."

Everyone has their own definitions of success and happiness.
Some people value success based on the amount of money and
power they have. Others look at it from a broader perspective
and claim that the most successful people are the ones who
make the biggest impact on the world while they are a part of it.

13

A "happy" person can be defined simply as someone who experiences positive emotions in their current state. Positive emotions like gratitude, joy, satisfaction, love, amusement, and hope can be attained differently, depending on the individual. In order to experience happiness over the long run, we must program our minds correctly and be ready for anything that life throws at us. In life, we all face hardships and are forced to overcome adversity at some point or another, but the happiest people are those who avoid negative emotions in even the darkest of times.

Whatever your definitions of these two words may be, it is certain that when you rise each morning, you aim to experience as much joy and prosperity as humanly possible.

Anyways, my name is Jeremy Bhandari. I hail from Ashland, Massachusetts. At the beginning of 2019, I decided to go around and interview some of the best athletes to ever grace this planet.

Rather than ask them about their astonishing statistics and accolades, I decided to take a different approach—an approach that I found would be beneficial to all. After speaking to these highly influential men and women, I broke down each conversation into what I call "The Keys to Making Life an Ease While Enjoying the Breeze." In writing terms, these are known as chapters.

I've included two poems to help distill some of the information in this book. If you don't already, I highly recommend writing poetry. Poetry is a therapeutic exercise and an incredible workout for your mind. When you write rhymes, you enhance your memory and improve cognitive performance in your brain. Scribbling down thoughts in your head while forming those ideas into a rhyming pattern is quite fulfilling.

Following each segment, you will find "Paramount Points." These are the main takeaways from each section and should be used not only as inspiration but also as daily reminders to keep yourself on track. Even after finishing the book, these ideas should be constantly reexamined to hold yourself accountable and keep yourself in the proper mindset. We all know how easy it is to get distracted in this world, so do yourself a favor and steadily brush up on these success secrets.

With that said, I give you *Trust the Grind*. While I can't make any guarantees, I can promise you one thing: after reading this story, you will undoubtedly be in a better position to identify your true purpose and live a life of full satisfaction than if you didn't pick up this book.

As always, be great, and avoid hate.

The First Time I Met Dr. Seuss

The first time I met Dr. Seuss,
I brought a notepad that I knew I would put to use,
At this point, Seuss was in his prime,
Teaching the youth how to read and rhyme,

I was obsessed with Green Eggs and Ham,
Hoping one day I would run into Sam-I-am
But meeting the creator of the Grinch was cool enough
And there he was, possessing a beard with days of scruff.

"Hello, Mr. Seuss, I am a huge fan of your books,
Your diction is exceptional, and I love the hooks!"
"Why thank you, young boy," he said with a smile,
"It's not every day a little kid compliments my style.

I see you brought some paper with you.
Would you like an autograph? Who should I make it out to?"
"To be honest sir, your signature would be neat,
But this paper is going to help me accomplish a feat.

See, we have a poem due next week in school,
And I thought I would ask for some help. Is that cool?"
"Sure thing, boy," he said with conviction,
"Is the poem going to be one of fact or fiction?"

"Fiction sir, and to earn a gold star,
I was thinking of making it about a fast car."
"Great idea son, a speedy car is unique,
Have you written anything down? May I take a quick peek?"

"Well, I decided that he will be driving in the rain,
But other than that, my ideas have been pretty plain."
"Adding in the weather was a smart move.
Here, let me offer some advice to help you get in a groove.

Let's step away from the car and the rainy day.
What overarching message are you trying to portray?
Every poem should be used as a learning tool.
Here is how we can make this poem rule:

I got to where I'm at in my career by setting goals
So let's talk about how important they are to educate young souls.
A life without goals is like a car without wipers on a rainy day—
Moving forward in life with no clear vision, and constant disarray.
However, when we write down our goals and say them out loud,
We stay focused and make our families real proud.
When the car in our story states his future desires,
He will add on his wipers and get some fresh new tires.

So even on days when nothing is going right,
The car's wipers will make sure he keeps a clean sight.
Now along with writing down my thoughts,
Write down a goal! Heck, write lots and lots!

Setting goals allows us to move forward with ease,
And constantly reviewing them is one of the keys.
So good luck with your poem and your cool made-up car.
Take this advice with you, and you'll go real far."

CHAPTER ONE

Set Goals

"The goal that kept me motivated throughout my baseball career was getting to the big leagues and playing with the best players in the world."

As a kid, Chipper Jones certainly set small goals like making the high school team as an eighth grader, but reaching the MLB was always his main focus.

Growing up in Pierson, Florida, the renowned Fern Capital of the World, Jones knew at a very young age that growing and selling fancy greenery was not as fun as hitting fastballs. His father, Larry Jones, was the head coach of the baseball team at Pierson Taylor High School, which allowed Chipper to be introduced to the game before he could even swing a bat. No, seriously. As a young boy, Chipper would stand in front of the family's wooden garage, holding a thirty-three-inch piece of PVC pipe about two inches thick and would hack away at the tennis balls his dad would pitch to him.

Although Larry grew up in Virginia, his favorite player was New York Yankees superstar Mickey Mantle. Mantle, a National Baseball Hall of Famer who won three MVP Awards and was named to the American League All-Star team twenty times, is arguably the greatest switch-hitter in MLB history. Once Chipper started crushing the ball onto the saran covering the ferns on the family farm, his father had him start practicing from the other side of the plate in hopes of developing the next Mickey Mantle.

Even when his dad wasn't around, Chipper was focused on his lofty goal of playing in the Show. Those who lived within the neighborhood would often see Chipper throwing tennis balls against a wall by himself, eager to perfect his fielding skills. Overly invested and on a mission, baseball was always on Chipper's mind. "When you grow up in a baseball family," Chipper said in a 1997 interview with *The Atlanta Constitution*, "It's all you're talking about at the dinner table, on the ride to school. It was always baseball."

As Chipper grew older, Larry and Lynne Jones, Larry's wife and Chipper's mother, saw something special brewing with their only child. In a Little League district playoff game, squaring off against one of the top teams in the nation, Altamont Springs, Chipper hit three home runs.

When he was in eighth grade, Chipper participated in a baseball clinic at Valencia Community College, an event where young players had the opportunity to showcase their talent in front of MLB scouts. After the clinic, George Zuraw, who at the time was a scout for the Cincinnati Reds, informed Chipper's dad that "Your son has a baseball future—a real future."

Larry worked closely with Chipper on the physical part of the game, while Lynne put an emphasis on the psychology aspect of being a competitor. In the same 1997 interview with *The Atlanta Constitution*, Chipper said, "She was always like, 'Don't you ever let any pitcher know that he's got you. Even if he strikes you out, you walk back to the dugout, and if you've got to talk a little smack to him, talk a little smack.' My mom's a tough little lady."

After his freshman year at Pierson Taylor, Chipper's parents decided to send their son off to The Bolles School, an esteemed private school that was two hours away from home. Not only would Bolles provide him with a better education, but the athletics were far superior to those of a public school. While, at the time, sending their son to a boarding school that was two hours away from home was a tough transition for the family, it was exactly what the young headliner needed. In our interview, Chipper said, "Sending me to Bolles in tenth grade was something that was critical in my development because I got to step on the bigger stage and they knew I needed that challenge."

As an upperclassman, Chipper's play on the diamond had MLB scouts and college recruiters in awe.

During his senior year, Chipper led the baseball team to the state championship game. That season, the Bolles star batted .488 with 10 doubles, 5 home runs, 25 RBI (or Runs Batted In), and 14 steals.

In the summer of 1990, Chipper put on more than just a graduation cap. In June, he became one step closer to reaching his childhood goal of playing with the best baseball players in the world. With the first pick in the 1990 MLB Draft, the Atlanta Braves selected Chipper Jones, making him the first Floridian to be chosen as the number one overall selection. He also became the thirteenth high school player to go first overall in the history of the MLB Draft. Following his selection, Atlanta Braves assistant vice president Paul Snyder, said, "Chipper is a blue-chip high school talent. The fact that he can switch-hit is a definite bonus, as is his tremendous speed." The term "blue-chip" is often used when referring to the stock market, or, when one alludes to someone, particularly an athlete, who has been touted as an elite prospect. The switch-hitting infielder quickly proved to the Braves franchise that they invested in the right player.

In 1991, Chipper, as a nineteen-year-old playing Class-A ball for the Macon Braves, hit .326 with 15 home runs and 40 steals in just 136 games. For those unfamiliar with how Minor League Baseball works, each professional baseball team has its own system of teams that span from AAA (triple A),

all the way down to rookie ball teams. The more "As" in the
class name, the higher the level of competition. Essentially
every player that you see in the MLB started his professional
career in the minors. Anyways, Chipper was named the South
Atlantic League's number one prospect and was promoted
to the Durham Bulls the following year. In Durham, Jones
collected 73 hits in seventy games. Seventy games were enough
for Atlanta's front office to advance Chipper to AA, where he
would finish out the 1992 season with the Greenville Braves. To
no surprise, Chipper tore it up, batting .346 with 9 home runs.
Although he played in just sixty-seven games, Chipper led the
team in triples with 11. In 1993, Chipper's childhood dream
came to fruition. After starting the season with the Richmond
Braves and leading the team in runs, hits, doubles, triples,
RBI, steals, and total bases, Atlanta called Chipper up to the
Major Leagues. On September 14, 1993, Jones collected his first
MLB hit, a single in the bottom of the seventh inning against
the Cincinnati Reds. He appeared in eight games at the end
of the regular season, recording 2 hits and 1 walk in four plate
appearances.

Since his sky-scraping objective of reaching the MLB had come
true, I was curious as to what kind of goals Chipper was setting
for himself at this point in his career. Once he became a full-
time starter in the Bigs, Chipper said, "I always wanted to be
considered a true and complete hitter. I wanted to hit .300, hit
30 tanks and drive in 100 runs, all while walking more than I
struck out. If I was doing those things, I knew I was helping my
team win." He also informed me that, when it came to goal-
setting, the Atlanta Braves legend "Focused on the immediate. I
knew that if I prepared from game to game and keep my goal of
being a 'tough at-bat' and not giving away at-bats, then I would
reach my goals at the end of the year." The idea of setting daily

objectives allowed Chipper to stay "ultra-focused on the now to produce the results [he] wanted long term."

An ACL injury caused Jones to miss the strike-shortened 1994 season, but in 1995, Chipper Jones had arrived.

In his first full season with the Braves, Jones led all MLB rookies in RBI (86) and runs scored (87). He was the first National League rookie since Dick Allen in 1964 to hit 20 home runs, 20 doubles, and score at least 85 runs.

In October, Jones helped the Atlanta Braves win their first World Series Championship since 1957, when the team was still in Milwaukee. Throughout the postseason, Chipper racked up 20 hits, which was good for second on the team. After the season, Atlanta Braves general manager John Schuerholtz was quoted saying that Jones is "more focused and serious than any young player I've ever been around."

At twenty-three years old, Jones was a World Series Champion and living out his childhood dream. Despite the immediate success, Jones raised the bar, setting even more exorbitant goals than before.

Following a solid 1996 campaign, Jones was interviewed in January 1997 by *The Atlanta Constitution*. During his conversation, he was asked by the reporter what his season goals would be for the upcoming season. Jones responded by saying, "Hit .320, .330, with 40 homers and 130 or 140 RBI."

Let's put some perspective on this. Since 1876, the first year of existence for the Braves franchise, only one player, Hank Aaron, had ever finished a season hitting .315 with 45 home runs and 100 RBI. The twenty-four-year-old Jones, using that confidence that his parents instilled in him, went on record to inform everyone he planned on putting up numbers, in the ballpark, that only one player in franchise history had ever achieved. Getting to the MLB was a lofty goal, but now aspiring to accomplish a feat that only one man in Braves history had done in the franchise's hundred plus years of existence? Impossible, right?

In 1999, Chipper Jones went on to win the NL MVP Award, hitting .319, with 45 home runs and 110 RBI. He became the first player in MLB history to hit .300 with 100 runs, 40 doubles, 100 RBI, 100 walks, and 20 steals, a stat line that has yet to be duplicated. In November of 1999, Hank Aaron told *The Atlanta Constitution*, "I don't think anyone was close to Chipper, as far as I was concerned, putting together a complete year in all categories." There are now two players in the Braves's storied franchise who finished a year batting at least .315, with 45 jacks, and 100 RBI: Hank Aaron and the sweet-swinging, switch-hitter from Pierson, Florida, Chipper Jones.

Following that season, Chipper, when asked about his remarkable '99 year, was quoted in the *Asheville Citizen Times* as saying, "It was an amazing year, but that was last year; this is this year." Appreciating the success, but always moving forward.

Remember that end-of-the-year goal of hitting .300 with 30 "tanks," 100 RBIs, and walking more than he struck out? Chipper fulfilled this objective in four straight seasons from 1998 to 2001.

After ten seasons in the MLB, Chipper Jones had shown he could do it all. His career average stood over .305, he had over 250 home runs, over 100 stolen bases, a career on-base percentage north of .400, and he even legged out over 25 triples. The only other player in MLB history to amass those gaudy statistics in their first ten seasons was Larry Jones's favorite player, Mickey Mantle.

As he entered his thirties, Jones continued to perform, even when others doubted. In a February 2004 interview with *The Atlanta Constitution*, Jones admitted he reads the papers and listens to the radio hosts, who had claimed Jones's career was headed downwards. Luckily for Chipper, the doubt was just fuel to the fire. Highly successful people like Chipper Jones don't let negative energy get in the way of pursuing their own goals. Later in that interview, Jones, who had just reached his target of bench pressing 320 pounds, spoke about the people who were uncertain he would be able to sustain the success he was having: "It's what motivates me to get in here [the weight room] and say okay, I'm going to show you."

In 2006, Chipper put together a stretch of fourteen straight games with at least one extra-base hit, a record that is tied with Paul Waner, who accomplished this feat in 1927. Brian McCann, Jones's teammate on the Braves, was asked about Chipper's magical streak. The catcher was quoted in *The Atlanta Constitution* saying, "What Chipper's doing right now is the craziest thing I've ever seen in my life."

The ensuing season, as a thirty-five-year-old, Jones batted .337 with 29 home runs and 102 RBI, while also leading the league in on-base and slugging percentage.

As we all know, Father Time is undefeated, especially when it comes to professional athletes, which was why I asked Chipper how his goals shifted, knowing he was in his mid-thirties. "As I grew older, I knew the power was going to decline a bit, so it made it easier to hit for a higher average and to take a different approach at the plate. I dedicated myself to using the whole field even more than I usually did and never gave away at-bats." Understanding that his body was getting older, instead of trying to crush 40 home runs, Chipper's goal was now to hit for a higher average.

At thirty-six years old, Chipper Jones hit a career-high .364 and won his first National League Batting Title while also leading the league in on-base percentage. To this date, only three players in MLB history, age thirty-six or older, posted a season with at least 150 hits, 20 home runs, and a batting average north of .360: Babe Ruth, Ted Williams, and Chipper Jones.

In 2012, Chipper retired from the game of baseball. He finished with 2,726 hits, 468 home runs, a .303 batting average, and a career on-base percentage of .401. Only three other players in the history of the sport have assembled those numbers: Babe Ruth, Mel Ott, and Stan Musial. Jones is one of two switch hitters (Mickey Mantle is of course the other) who hit at least 450 home runs while also getting on-base at least 40 percent of the time.

When I was digging through his statistics, I also noticed Chipper fared extremely well against some of the top pitchers in baseball history. He gave National Baseball Hall of Famer Randy Johnson absolute fits, hitting .349 with 6 home runs against the tall lefty. Against Curt Schilling, a 216-game winner in the MLB, Jones hit .303 with 4 long balls. In our interview, he told me, "I always loved facing the best. It made me work that much harder and focus that much more. Those types of guys always brought out the best of everything in me."

On January 24, 2018, Jones received the news that he would be getting inducted into the National Baseball Hall of Fame. While all of his personal success was remarkable, Jones made sure to never forget the two people who helped him accomplish his goals: his mom and dad. When I asked Chipper about the importance of having a good support system when one is pursuing their goals, he went into great detail explaining the positive effect his parents have had on him. "They are your foundation and give you unconditional love and support through the good and the bad. They keep you grounded, having you mow the lawn or get in the fernery no matter what successes or failures I had on the field. They ultimately shape you into the person you become."

Only two switch hitters in MLB history have hit at least 450 home runs while posting an on-base percentage better than .400: Chipper Jones and Mickey Mantle.

Nowadays, Chipper can be found spending time with family or hunting outside in the woods. He takes what he learned as a ballplayer and easily transitioned it to the outdoors. When I asked about the differences between baseball and hunting, Jones said "Honestly, there are a lot of similarities. You have to scout, work hard at staying committed, have discipline, and accept a lot of defeat in order to have success. You will certainly get lucky from time to time, as in baseball, but ultimately, you need to be dedicated to your goal and pursue it diligently."

As a parent, Chipper instills the same lessons that his mother and father taught him. "I simply want them to know that I will support them in whatever they do, as long as they commit to it and show me that they are going to work hard at whatever it might be. I try to simply teach them that hard work will always pay off, whether or not you get the desired results."

Chipper Jones finished his MLB career with 2,726 hits, 468 home runs, a .303 batting average, and an on-base percentage of .401. Only three other players in the history of the sport have assembled those numbers: Babe Ruth, Mel Ott, and Stan Musial.

When you think about Chipper Jones, appreciate the outlandish numbers, but try to zone in on the approach he has when it comes to setting goals. Throughout his life, he was never afraid to set colossal objectives. Even if they seemed unattainable to most and hadn't been accomplished in over a hundred years, Jones pursued his goals with persistence. By focusing on the immediate, on a game-to-game basis, Jones was able to do things on the diamond that we simply have never seen.

So be like Chipper. Set goals as high as humanly possible. Wake up each day with an approach. Block out any negative energy that might be in your way. Don't back down from the best. Appreciate those who are there to support you on your journey, and pass along what you have learned to the next ones in line.

If you want to be successful in life, saying your goals out loud or writing them down will automatically give you a better chance of achieving them.

Jack Canfield (author, motivational speaker, corporate trainer, and entrepreneur) dedicated an entire blog to the power of sharing your goals with others. Canfield references studies that investigated people attempting to shed a few pounds. The research revealed that the individuals who publicly mentioned their weight loss goals lost more weight than those who kept their aspirations to themselves.

So be like Chipper, and speak those ambitions into existence. A study conducted by Procedia Social and Behavioral Sciences concluded that basketball players who said motivational affirmations to themselves in the middle of games performed better than those who stayed silent. Gary Lupyan, researcher from the University of Wisconsin-Madison, asked individuals to rummage through a bunch of photos and look for an assigned one. According to the *New York Times*, "if they said the name or whatever object [was on the photo] out loud while looking, they tended to find the image faster." When talking to ourselves, we are internally improving our focus, which leads to better decision making, which will allow us to reach our goals at a faster rate.

This principle stands true with anything in life. The more we say out loud whatever it is we want, the better our chances become of achieving the said task.

You see, saying your goals out loud provides you with three things you otherwise would not have had if you kept them to yourself. Number one, the simple act of telling a friend, family member, or, in Chipper's case, a reporter, will give you more confidence. Second, you automatically become more accountable. People who you told will most likely follow up with you on the goal you promised to achieve, which, in turn, will cause you to internally work harder toward it. Third, you will have a better understanding of what you wish to conquer. Sometimes, we think we want something but are unsure exactly what that something entails. Often, people wish for more money, a nicer car, the ability to take a vacation, a better job, etc. By describing out loud the Lamborghini we want to drive, the managerial job we strive for, or even the beaches in Punta Cana, we signal to our brain exactly what we wish for our reality to look like.

Mark Murphy, bestselling author and founder and CEO of the research and consulting firm Leadership IQ, conducted a study of 4,690 men and women. In his findings, Murphy concluded that fewer than 20 percent of the participants said their goals were "always" written down vividly. People who vividly wrote down their goals, or were able to picture them with ease, were reported to be 1.2 to 1.4 times more likely to fulfill their intention.

In another study, Dr. Gail Matthews, a psychology professor at the Dominican University in California, divided 267 men and women into two groups. One group consisting of individuals who wrote down their goals, and the other group was made up of those who did not. No shocker here—those who scribbled down their objectives were 42 percent more likely to achieve them.

Scientifically speaking, all of our brains have a left and right hemisphere. When you ponder something that you desire, you turn on the right hemisphere. However, when you think about this desire *and* scribble it down, you also activate your left hemisphere—the logic-based side of your brain. Simply writing down your goals activates a logical part of your brain that otherwise would not have been tapped into had you only thought about those goals.

New York Times science writer John Tierney and psychologist Roy F. Baumeister researched the success rate of when our unconscious mind propels our conscious mind to make an agenda or set a future intention.

Whether it is a to-do list or a catalog of goals and aspirations, if we physically draw up a course of action, we will naturally get an inkling of achievement, even if the goal or task has not been met. In *Willpower: Rediscovering the Greatest Human*

Strength, Tierney and Baumeister note that our brains are naturally wired to continuously berate our conscious thoughts with any unmet endeavors that we set for ourselves. This idea is known as the Zeigarnik effect, which is, by GoodTherapy's definition, a psychological phenomenon describing a tendency to remember interrupted or incomplete tasks or events more easily than tasks that have been completed. However, that definition was created in the 1920s. Further research on the Zeigarnik effect by Tierney and Baumeister inferred that our unconscious mind cannot develop "a plan" on its own, which is why it begs our conscious mind to do so. Once we set up a future opportunity and pair it with a fixed deadline, we will instinctively get a sense of attainment.

Even if we have yet to reach our objectives, scribbling them down will force our brains to focus on them until they are reached. I am going to say this again: please write down the goals and tasks you want to achieve as clearly as possible.

Jot them down, share them with others, and constantly chat with yourself about whatever it is you yearn for. Doing one or all three of these methods is scientifically proven to improve your chances, so give it a try.

Paramount Points

- Set all types of goals (ex. daily goals, short-term goals, and long-term goals). Creating goals gives you a reason to get up every day and seek greatness.

- Have the valor to speak your goals out loud, no matter how superlative they appear.

- Writing down your goals and aspirations will help you stay focused and internally put you in a good position to be successful.

- NEVER shy away from those who are willing to help you while you are on your mission. Be extremely cognizant if another individual chooses to take time out of their own life to assist you.

- Wake up each day and remind yourself of your goals. Writing them down has proven to help, so take ten seconds and jot down *exactly* what you want. Be precise and include every single detail.

CHAPTER TWO

Develop Discipline

"It wasn't about money. It wasn't about headlines. I wanted to be the best. I wanted to win, and that's why I played."

In life, in order to reach some sort of success, you must have self-discipline. Self-discipline is defined as "the ability to control one's feelings and overcome one's weaknesses; the ability to pursue what one thinks is right despite temptations to abandon it," by Google dictionary. However, self-discipline is not something you magically attain as you grow. As a kid growing up in San Francisco going all the way to the Naismith Memorial Basketball Hall of Fame, Jason Kidd's story is one that encapsulates self-discipline and everything that comes with it.

In grade school, we were all asked what we wanted to be when we grew up. Some marveled at the idea of being an actor while others dreamed of being a firefighter, astronaut, or teacher. By the second grade, all Jason Kidd wanted to do was be a professional athlete. While sitting in class, Kidd would draw himself on a court, making sure to include whatever jersey number he aspired to wear. When I spoke with Jason, he recalled "role-playing how they were going to introduce my name when I took the field or came onto the court." When it was recess time, he envisioned himself as Magic Johnson or Julius "Dr. J" Erving.

To work toward this walloping dream, Jason spent nearly all of his free time playing sports. Even on days when he wasn't up for another soccer practice, he persevered. His parents taught him what commitment meant, and if they could work all day and still make sure Jason was on time for every practice, the least he could do was return the favor by giving it his all.

As he grew older, Jason shifted the majority of his focus to basketball. He would spend countless hours on the court, working on all aspects of his game. Kidd noted, "I was always traveling to play in a basketball tournament somewhere. I thought that was just the norm as a kid growing up. I loved to play. I would play anywhere." By the time he was in middle school, Jason's passion for the game had helped mold him into one of the best players in all of California. Still, that wasn't good enough for Kidd, who recalls attending a basketball camp in Kansas while he was a seventh grader. It was an opportunity for young Jason to play with some of the most talented high school players in the nation. He said, "To be the best, I wanted to play against the best throughout the country."

His eventual high school basketball coach, Frank LaPorte, recalls the first time he saw Jason at a summer youth tournament. In a 1991 interview for the San Francisco Chronicle, LaPorte said, "He did some things out there that even amazed coaches. One approached me and wondered if he was a junior [in high school]. I said, 'No he's a freshman.' Everybody knew. As an eighth grader, Jason Kidd was the talk of the town."

Because of LaPorte's vision and belief in Kidd's abilities, Jason, a freshman in high school, was put in front of cameras to do media interviews. LaPorte knew the sky was the limit for his new star player and wanted to get him comfortable and prepared for what he will have to go through for years to come.

By the time Kidd was an upperclassman, all of America had started to take notice. As a junior, he finished the year averaging 25 points, 12 rebounds, 8 assists, and 6 steals per game. After practices, Kidd would set aside time to open up fan mail. Kidd, when asked about the fan mail, told the *LA Times* in 1991, "Younger kids mostly write and tell me I am their hero. They tell me they're my number one fan and that they want to be my friend."

St. Joseph's gym had a seating capacity of just eight hundred, but, because of the attention on Kidd, games against rival schools had to be played in larger venues. In a January win over Oakland Bishop O'Dowd, Kid dropped 35 points and hauled down 11 rebounds in front of a crowd of five thousand at Cal State Hayward. This doesn't include the hundreds of fans who were shut out at the door.

Media requests for interviews with the St. Joseph star were so excessive that Coach LaPorte had to stop answering his phone and returning texts.

With Kidd's incredible play, Alameda St Joseph, with a record of 30 wins to 3 losses, made it all the way to the state championship to square off against Los Angeles Fremont. Up to this point, Southern California teams had dominated the Northern California squads in the state final, having won nine straight contests.

Early in the game, it looked like that trend would continue. Fremont led by 6 at half-time and racked up a 10-point lead late in the third quarter. However, St. Joseph's 10 to 0 run had the score knotted up. It was then Kidd's time to shine in front of nearly fifteen thousand fans and show why he was considered the nation's top player. In the final three minutes of the state championship, Kidd, who was playing with 4 fouls, notched in 7 points, 3 steals, and 2 assists. He would finish the contest with a game-high 25 points, 8 rebounds, 7 steals, 4 assists, and 1 block. Kidd's epic performance gave St. Joseph their first state title in school history. In a post-game interview with the *LA Times* in 1991, Fremont coach Sam Sullivan said the obvious: "Kidd is a fantastic ballplayer who carried his team and won them a championship."

Following the game, hundreds of avid, hopped-up fans waited outside the coliseum for Kidd's autograph. It was an exciting time for the Bay Area. Joe Montana, Jerry Rice, and the San Francisco 49ers had just won Super Bowl XXIV. Rickey Henderson, Dave Stewart, Mark McGwire, and Dennis Eckersley had pioneered the Oakland Athletics and won the 1989 World Series. And now, there was eighteen-year-old Jason Kidd, as popular as anyone in the state.

Naismith Memorial Basketball Hall of Famer Gary Payton, a native of the Bay Area, summarized it best in a 2018 interview with *ESPN*. "Joe Montana was doing the things in the '80s—winning Super Bowls," Payton said. "I had left [for college] in '86, and then J came in and all of the sudden, they [Montana and Kidd] were the biggest things in the Bay Area at the time."

Despite all this attention, Kidd stayed grounded. In our interview, he said, "Whenever I saw the newspapers, I just read about Joe Montana and how successful he was as a professional. That's what I paid attention to. It wasn't so much me being in the newspaper. I focused on the superstars in the Bay Area that I wanted to be like."

In the summer following the state championship, Kidd was given the opportunity to practice with the Golden State Warriors. Playing with guys like Tim Hardaway, Mitch Richmond, and Chris Mullin, Kidd was quickly humbled. "As someone who just won a state title, you feel like you're on cloud nine. I got to see I still had a long way to go."

Eager to improve his game, Kidd also spent that summer practicing with Gary Payton, who was five years older than

Jason and a member of the Seattle SuperSonics. Rather than taking it easy on the teen, Payton showed no mercy. After one day of working out with the former number two overall pick in the 1990 NBA draft, Kidd went home to his parents and cried. Payton did not let him score one basket and, in typical Gary Payton fashion, talked a lot of trash, constantly reminding Kidd that he was still just a high schooler. Kidd recalls the advice his parents offered as they looked at their son with tears in his eyes: "You gotta go back. You're not just gonna sit here."

From then on, Kidd approached each practice with a positive attitude. "Showing how far away I was just made me that much hungrier," he said. The goal of becoming a professional athlete was still his focus, and surrounding himself with the best was an easy way to elevate his game. Spending time with people who are better in a particular field causes one to push themselves harder while also focusing on the fundamental aspects of the challenge ahead.

As a senior, with thousands of "Jason Kidd" jerseys and posters being sold at school, Kidd did not disappoint his fan club. While averaging 25 points, 10 assists, 7 rebounds, and 7 steals, Kidd led St. Joseph to another state championship. To add to his trophy case, Kidd received the Naismith Award, an award given to the nation's top high school player and was named the state's player of the year for the second time in a row.

With dozens of schools begging for his talents, Kidd decided to stay in-state and attend the University of California, Berkeley.

Despite coming off two straight losing seasons, Cal was immediately back in national attention. thanks to their new star. During his freshman season, Kidd averaged 13 points, 7.7 assists, 4.9 rebounds, and led the country with 110 steals. Kidd set an NCAA record for most steals by a freshman. He was named National Freshman of the Year, while also earning a spot on the All-Pac-10 team.

Kidd thrived on the biggest stage: the NCAA tournament. In the opening round against LSU, he had 16 points, 7 rebounds, 7 assists, and 5 steals. There was no bucket bigger than his game-winning basket, which is now referred to as the "pretzel shot," a name coined by LSU coach Dale Brown.

Following the contest, according to a 1993 *LA Times* article, Brown claimed that the sixth-seeded Cal Bears had no chance to beat the third-seeded Duke Blue Devils, who were coming off back-to-back National Championships. Brown also added that Kidd would be no match for Duke's All-American point guard, Bobby Hurley.

With under three minutes to play in Cal's second-round game against Duke, trailing 77–76, Kidd attempted to pass the ball inside to a teammate, but it was batted away. Rather than giving up on the play, Kidd hustled to the ball, and, while falling down after being fouled by Grant Hill, put up a shot that bounced off the backboard and directly through the net. He went on to make his free throw, giving Cal a 79–77 lead. A lead that the Bears never gave back. Cal's 82–77 victory gave the Bears their first Sweet 16 appearance since 1960.

The nation's best freshmen finished the game with 11 points, 14 assists (Cal record for an NCAA tournament game), 8 rebounds, and 4 steals. The performance earned him a spot on the cover of *Sports Illustrated* just two days later. Although Cal was defeated by Kansas in the following round, the Bears' season was a success.

As a sophomore in the ensuing season, Kidd continued to excel. In a January game against Stanford, Kidd had 18 assists, which is still a school record for most assists in a game. He finished the season with 272 assists, which was not only the most in a season by a Cal player, but also stands as a Pac-10 conference record. He was named 1994 Pac-10 Player of the Year. Following his impressive campaign, Kidd declared for the NBA draft, forgoing his junior and senior season.

Despite playing just two years, Kidd racked up 204 steals, a program record, and the most ever by a Pac-10/12 player. In California program history, there have been 5 total triple-doubles to date. Kidd had 4 of them. In 2004, Kidd's number 5 jersey was retired by the program.

Kidd was selected second overall in the 1994 NBA draft by the Dallas Mavericks. After an impressive rookie season, leading all first-year players with 7.7 assists per game, Kidd shared the 1995 NBA Rookie of the Year Award with Grant Hill of the Detroit Pistons. The following season, he made his first All-Star team and finished the year averaging 16.6 points, 9.7 assists, and 6.8 rebounds.

From 1997 to 2001, no player had more assists than the San Francisco native. During that span, Kidd made three more All-Star teams and led the NBA in assists in three straight seasons. In 2001, after stints with the Mavericks and Suns, Kidd was sent to the New Jersey Nets, a team that was coming off a dreadful 26–56 record.

Eager to shift the culture in a positive direction, Kidd set the tone early on during training camp when he dove for a ball in a summer practice. "Every possession means something," he said. "I'm out here to compete and win." While showing leadership skills, Kidd, already one of the premier assist-men in the league, focused on his jumper. When I asked Kidd how he went about molding his shot, I was anything but surprised with his answer. He said, "I shot thousands of shots [per day] and worked on my technique."

Kidd would head to the practice facility early, working on his approach as the rest of the team piled in. After technique work, Kidd gave me the rest of the rundown for the day: "Then you have the team practice. Then after practice, now you're working on your corners. Start to work on your distance. Shooting from different spots on the floor, taking shots that you would get in the game."

While all this work may get exhausting, Kidd reminded me that you have to put in the work and believe in what you do in order to see positive results. "There's going to be days where everything feels perfect, but the ball just doesn't go in. Are you going to believe in what you're doing is right and stick with it? Or are you going to try and change it? I had to trust that we were doing the right thing and it paid off."

During his first season with the Nets, Kidd averaged 14.7 points, 9.9 assists, 7.3 rebounds, and led all NBA players with 175 steals, which had me asking him how the heck he was so good defensively.

Kidd responded, "It starts with your want. You gotta want to do something that most people don't." While the majority of players consider playing lockdown defense, "dirty work," Kidd relished the idea of trying to shut down the opposing team's best player. He said, "I watched a lot of film. I studied the opponent. Not just the guy I would be guarding, but also the other guys. Just in case there was a switch." Kidd talked about breaking down film of guys like Muggsy Bogues, Reggie Miller, and Michael Jordan. When he brought up Mike, Kidd was quick to mention "that [Michael's] file was really small because he was just too good." Kidd also said that film was something he started to study back when he was in high school. No wonder he currently ranks as the nation's all-time high school leader in steals.

Kidd had transformed the Nets, leading them to a 52–30 regular-season record and finishing runner-up to Tim Duncan in MVP voting. During the postseason, Kidd performed how he always does in big moments, leading New Jersey all the way to the NBA Finals before ultimately falling to the Los Angeles Lakers. In his twenty playoff games, Kidd scored over 300 points, brought down over 150 rebounds, and tallied up over 175 assists. In the history of basketball, only two other players, Magic Johnson (1990–91) and Lebron James (2017–18), have accomplished that feat in a single postseason run.

The next season, Kidd averaged a career-high 18.7 points and had the Nets right back in the NBA Finals. Although they fell short for the second season in a row, losing in six games to the San Antonio Spurs, Jason Kidd had changed the culture in New Jersey and proved he was a winner.

In 2011, at age thirty-seven, Kidd was finally able to hoist the Larry O'Brien Championship Trophy. As the starting point guard for the Dallas Mavericks, Kidd and his teammates defeated the Miami Heat in six games to capture the franchise's first NBA championship. In game three of the NBA Finals, Kidd recorded 10 assists, becoming the oldest player over the last thirty years to have a 10-assist game in the NBA finals.

Jason Kidd ended his career as a ten-time All-Star, five-time All-NBA First-Team member, and a nine-time NBA All-Defensive Team member. He currently ranks second in NBA history in career assists and steals, while also holding onto tenth place in 3-point field goals made. Only two players in the history of the sport finished their career with at least 15,000 points, 10,000 assists, and 5,000 rebounds. One of them is Jason Kidd, and the other is the man who Kidd often mimicked as a child on the playgrounds: Magic Johnson. In 2018, Kidd was inducted into the Naismith Memorial Basketball Hall of Fame, going down in history as one of the best point guards the game has seen.

At the end of our interview, I asked Jason his thoughts on what he believes are the keys to self-discipline. Obviously, in order to be considered "disciplined" you must identify what you are trying to accomplish. Ever since he was a kid, Jason was focused on becoming the best possible basketball player and would do whatever it took to win. Whether it was breaking down film of his opponent or shooting thousands of jumpers a day, Kidd was committed to the craft.

Not only do they have insane work ethics, self-disciplined people make taking care of their bodies their first priority. Kidd credits getting the right amount of rest and eating the proper foods as the main reasons he was able to stay in the league for so long and perform at a high level. He always ate oatmeal for breakfast, and Kidd firmly believed in taking a nap before the game to physically and mentally rest. Part of staying disciplined is making sure you are locked-in and alert at all times. In order to maintain a heightened focus, you must get a suitable amount of rest. So if you need to, be like Jason and mix in a nap.

For five years, researchers from the University Hospital of Lausanne, Switzerland, followed 3,462 individuals, all between thirty-five and seventy-five years old and noted that people who napped once or twice a week actually lowered their risk of suffering from any sort of cardiovascular disease. The academics also concluded that these individuals were 48 percent less likely than non-nappers to endure a heart attack, stroke, or suffer from heart failure.

Everyone has that family member, friend, or coworker who, no matter what the situation, finds a way to complain. You know, the ones that swear they have worse luck than anyone on the planet and are convinced that someone is out to get them. Well, when it comes to building self-discipline in life, the more negativity you are around, the less productivity you will generate.

Jason credited a lot of his success to surrounding himself with the right individuals. He said, "When you're around someone or around people who are doing the right thing, that makes it a lot easier for you to do the right thing." When Jason spent that summer practicing with NBA stars, he was able to pick their brains and get a first-person look at what it takes to be a professional.

It's time to put your ego aside and seek out individuals who are smarter and more experienced than you. While you may feel inadequate or feeble at first, much like Jason when he first stepped up against Gary Payton, I can promise that hard work pays off and that there is no better way to grow in a particular field or area than spending time with those who have already walked the path that you are pursuing.

For those who aren't blessed to be in an atmosphere with high performers in the department that they hope to specialize in, Jason recommends writing in a diary—something that was suggested to him during his time with the Phoenix Suns. In this diary, Kidd would document when things were going well and when things weren't so pretty. That way, he was able to better prepare himself for when future events arise.

"You have to write things down," he said. "Things aren't always going to go well. You can go back at your notes and look back at the time when you were playing at a very high level. [I can see] what was I doing during this time, what was I eating, what was I doing on the court, what was going on in my life, so you can always reflect. When it's 60 games in [of the NBA season] and I'm tired, I look back at the book to see what I did last year during this time to get over the hump." Whether it was the ups and downs of the rigorous NBA season or far-fetched goals he wished to accomplish, Kidd made note of it all.

In our goal-setting chapter, we saw the power of writing down our dreams, aspirations, and even simple tasks that we wanted to get done. Jason Kidd's story is a living example of the benefits of taking time out of your day to document your journey, manifesting that this simple action is a pivotal step in attaining long-term success.

Only two players in NBA history have scored over 15,000 points, corralled 5,000 rebounds, and dished out 10,000 assists: Earvin "Magic" Johnson and Jason Kidd.

After talking with Jason, I purchased my own diary. Any time I felt a day went well, I would make sure to jot down the steps I took during that day for it to be a success. Whether it was the food I ate, the people I spoke with, how I managed my time, or even the thoughts I generated inside my head, I included it all. On days that I struggled or encountered moments where I came up short, I went into full detail as to why the particular situation played out as it did and how I can improve the next time it arises.

The concept of writing in a diary is now a staple for me. Think about it. Life happens so fast, making it impossible to remember everything that goes on. With a diary, you give yourself the ability to reflect on your personal life, which ultimately helps prepare yourself for a brighter future.

While I was hoping to learn a little bit about swag from Jason (if you haven't seen his bleach blonde hair cut from his Phoenix days, please check it out), getting the chance to talk about discipline and absorbing ways to ultimately better myself is just as good.

Discipline is, by far, the most common trait adopted by all successful people. If you aspire to be in the top 1 percent, you must do what only 1 percent of people are willing to do. While breaking down videos of your opponents in high school or taking thousands of jump shots a day may not be the most glamourous way to spend time, it was how Jason Kidd separated himself from the pack.

Self-discipline is attained by training your mind to solely focus on what you feel is important in order to achieve your goals. Someone who wants to lose weight must develop the discipline to eat strong, healthy foods rather than those filled with sugar. If you wish to get all As on your report card, you must discipline yourself and spend extra time studying while others take part in activities that will not benefit them in the long run.

Beyond self-reflection, journals can be utilized as a way to mightily improve our efficiency. As you know, when we write things down, we automatically give ourselves a better chance to accomplish any task or goal. For further emphasis, here is an examination on doodling in the classroom.

In 1996, Beesley and Apthorp conducted a study to see the links between strong note-taking and overall success of college students. They were eager to see if writing down notes led to stronger retention of the information at hand. According to the Association for Supervision and Curriculum Development, the group who took notes performed better on tests than those who chose not to record the information during lectures. The researchers also found that the note-takers actually outperformed the control group who reviewed the lecture annotations but did not physically write them down.

In 2012, James and Engelhardt constructed a study using fifteen children in Indiana. The boys and girls were asked to write, trace, or type out letters while their brains were scanned. The researchers, according to *Trends in Neuroscience and Education*, identified that scripting the letters triggered more brain regions than typing them on a computer.

Even in the digital age, there is still something special about writing things down. Not only are you more prone to retain the information you write, but your brain is literally energized in ways that aren't possible unless you put pen to paper. So each day, write down what you would like to accomplish. It only takes a minute and automatically increases your chances of getting things done.

Paramount Points

- Boost your benchmark by surrounding yourself with individuals who have a successful track record in the field that you wish to excel in.

- Identify what it takes to be successful in your coveted field. Part of becoming a self-disciplined individual is grasping what it takes to be prosperous

- There will be days when you are tired, not in the mood, and shots just aren't falling, but KEEP GOING.

- Purchase a journal, and use it to track your journey.

- If you want to be in the 1 percent of people, you must do what only 1 percent of people are willing to do.

CHAPTER THREE

Stay Driven

"People think that I'm a four or five-star recruit, but I wasn't. I didn't start on the varsity team until my junior year. My peers around me—they were better athletes than I was."

The first son to Marilyn Heard, Terrell Owens grew up in Alexander City, Alabama. He was raised by his mother and grandmother. When Marilyn was young, Alice, Terrell's grandmother, raised her in a relatively restrictive environment. Marilyn was not allowed to play with the other children in the neighborhood and was forced to come straight home after school. Had she broken any of her mother's rules, you can bet there were heavy repercussions.

Terrell was brought up no differently. He was whipped regularly and was not allowed to spend time with friends. There were often times where Owens would glance across the street and see his friends shooting hoops or throwing a ball around, but, because of his firm, unbending grandmother, Owens couldn't do more than observe the kids having fun. Despite this, Terrell loved his grandmother, who taught him strength and truly made him into the person he has become today. In his emotional Pro Football Hall of Fame speech, Owens made sure the first people he thanked were his mother and late grandmother.

Ever since he was young, Owens was heavily active in sports. He played baseball and basketball, swam, ran track, and, of course, played football. However, the man who ranks third all-time in receiving touchdowns was not always the undisputed best player on the field.

As a high schooler, Owens did not regularly start on the varsity football team at Benjamin Russell High School until his senior year. In fact, during his junior year, Terrell was given the opportunity to get his first career start simply because the starter at his position got sick on the day of the game.

When he was in the lineup, a lanky Owens, wearing a jersey that appeared oversized because of his lack of muscle, turned into a solid receiver for the Wildcats.

While no big-name college football program had reached out to recruit Terrell, the University of Tennessee at Chattanooga had taken notice. Not in a traditional way, however. While the Chattanooga coaches were breaking down film of one of Terrell's teammates, they noticed the athletic Owens making a few plays and decided to offer him a scholarship.

Not only did he play football for the Mocs, but Owens was also the first man off the bench for the basketball team. During his senior year, Owens ran track after the coach invited him last minute. He went on to compete in the 4 x 100 relay at the NCAA championship.

However, it was on the football field where Owens truly made a name for himself. Despite the team winning just thirteen games during his four years at Chattanooga, Owens starred for the Mocs. He led the team in receiving yards in three straight seasons (1993–95) and, despite often being double covered by defenders, currently ranks third in the program's history with 19 receiving touchdowns. So, how did a kid who didn't regularly start on his high school team turn into a collegiate star? Simply put by Owens: "My desire, my dedication, and my discipline."

For the majority of students, college vacation breaks are a glorious time. You get to go home to family and friends, catch up on some sleep, and not worry about dedicating much of your time to academics.

While all of his peers used the summer and winter breaks as vacation time away from the university, Owens decided to stay on campus. Coming from a lower-income family, it was tough for Owens to travel back to Alabama. Plus, he understood that there was nothing going on in Alexander City.

Eager to improve on his game, Terrell would beg his coaches for the keys to the gym. He said, "I wanted to get myself bigger, stronger, faster." Despite no one being around to spot him, Owens grinded in the weight room. Bench press, squats, free weights, you name it. Sometimes struggling to get the bar off his chest during heavy workouts, Owens looked at this time in his life as nothing but positive. "Going through hard times is what made me stronger," he said. "I took advantage of being on the campus by myself. I did the hard, grind work when no one was watching." Owens later went on to state, "I wasn't going to allow my circumstances to dictate my future."

By his junior year at Chattanooga, Owens's dominant play was catching the eyes of NFL scouts. Owens, who weighted maybe 170 pounds in high school, was now turning into a physical beast at six foot, three inches and 213 pounds. He was a versatile talent, alternating between playing wide receiver, running back, and quarterback, while also returning kicks.

Along with his football abilities, teams relished the fact that he was a multi-sport athlete. One team in particular, the San Francisco 49ers, really liked what they saw in Owens. So much so that they decided to select him with the eighty-ninth overall pick in the 1996 NFL draft. Terrell was the twelfth receiver chosen in the draft, but he wasn't concerned about any of that. In fact, Owens was ecstatic. Not only was he now a professional football player, but he would also be sharing the field with his idol, 49ers receiver Jerry Rice. After Owens was drafted, 49ers receivers coach Larry Kirksey noted, "He's a big, strong athlete who plays faster than his speed. He's raw in some areas, but that's what we're here for."

It didn't take long for San Francisco fans to get familiar with Owens. Following the 49ers' initial practice in training camp, Niners defensive backs were going around softly asking reporters, "Hey, who's number fifteen?" The answer, of course, was Owens. When the second minicamp was over, it was clear that the rookie needed immediate playing time. Although he was forced to learn over two hundred passing plays, after having only ten in college, Owens kept his head in the books, worked hard after practice, and continued to stay focused.

In the 49ers' preseason opener, Owens knocked down two Denver Broncos with one block while also catching three passes for 44 yards. In the second game, he led all players with 87 receiving yards. In an interview with the *San Francisco Chronicle*, the 49ers' offensive coordinator Marc Trestman noted that Terrell was "dedicated and passionate about doing the job. We're fortunate to have Jerry ahead of him so we can work him in and see how he handles different situations."

Through the first six regular-season games, Owens was targeted only seven times, hauling in three passes for a total of 32 yards. However, after a season-ending injury to Niners' wide receiver J.J. Stokes, who needed surgery on his dislocated wrist, Terrell slid into the starting lineup. In game number seven against the Cincinnati Bengals, Owens caught four passes for 94 yards, including a fourth-quarter, 45-yard touchdown that tied the game and set up the 49ers' quarterback Steve Young's game-winning run. The following week, against the Houston Oilers, Owens hauled in the game-winning 20-yard touchdown pass.

While 49ers fans were elated with how their rookie receiver was playing, Scott McKinney, the director of sports information at Chattanooga, knew it was only a matter of time for Terrell to succeed in the NFL. During the Mocs' preseason two-a-day practices, the players ran multiple 40-yard sprints. On any given practice, the athletes would usually run as many as fifty sprints during the hot, dry August days. McKinney would watch in awe as Owens would not only finish his sprints but also yell out words of inspiration and run aside his teammates who were struggling to keep up.

Following these harsh practices, Owens would spend an hour and a half in the weight room. In an interview with the *San Francisco Chronicle*, McKinney noted, "If Jerry Rice is the hardest working guy in the NFL, the second hardest working guy is Terrell Owens. His workout regimen would kill a common man. I mean kill him dead." McKinney would go on to say "He is one of the nicest kids to ever walk on campus, football player or non-player. He's almost too good to be true. He's Ken Griffey Jr., Walter Payton, and Forrest Gump all rolled into one."

Not only did McKinney speak highly of Owens, but Steve Young also appreciated the production that Owens had brought to the team. He said, "He's won two games in a row. He's going to be a force because of his strength. He's the consummate receiver, like Jerry Rice, with the strength to get off the line of scrimmage, get open, catch the ball and really shed defensive backs." Predicting the future is something Young can add to his résumé.

Owens would wrap up his rookie season with 520 receiving yards and 4 touchdowns. The following year, in the 49ers season opener, Jerry Rice, San Francisco's star receiver, tore the anterior cruciate and medial collateral ligaments in his knee after being ripped down by Warren Sapp of the Tampa Bay Buccaneers. Rice was forced to miss the next fourteen weeks, giving Owens a chance to shine.

Just like he took advantage of his high school teammate getting sick and Stokes going down his rookie year, Owens thrived in his new role. He went on to lead the 49ers in receptions (60), receiving yards (936) and receiving touchdowns (8). It was now clear that if you want to win, you need to give Terrell Owens the football. In 1998, with Rice back in the lineup, Owens continued to flourish. He had his first career 1,000-yard receiving season and led the 49ers with 14 receiving touchdowns.

When I spoke with Terrell, I was interested to know what his life was like during his first few years in the NFL. While he had a taste of what it is like to be on top, Owens was never content. He said, "I wasn't satisfied with the little success I had. I wanted to be the best I could be." I later asked about how he spent his time away from football during the late '90s. In his first three seasons with the 49ers, Owens lived with his grandmother. During the offseason, he would train, jump rope, and run 40-yard dashes in the street right outside of his grandmother's house. The professional football star said, "I would run from my home to the high school, workout with the high school team while they were doing two-a-days, and then go back and do my own workout."

During the season, Tuesday was usually the day off for the 49ers team. However, as you can probably tell at this point, there were no days off for Owens, who would head down to Oakland to play pickup basketball with the local residents at a nearby 24-Hour Fitness. This, of course, was to work on his lateral quickness. A budding star in the NFL who would spend his off days playing hoops and summers training outside of his grandma's house, Owens never lost focus of trying to be not just good, but legendary.

To prolong his career, Owens took exceptional care of his health. T.O.'s breakfast consisted of egg whites, oatmeal, and either a chicken or turkey sausage. He stayed away from fried foods and, although never a big drinker, made sure from 2000 onward to not consume any alcohol during the season.

From 2000 to 2002, Owens made three straight Pro Bowls and was selected First-Team All-Pro at the end of each season. During that three-year span, Owens led all NFL players with 42 receiving touchdowns. After another solid season in 2003, it was time for a new chapter in T.O.'s football life. In March 2004, Owens became a member of the Philadelphia Eagles, who were coming off back-to-back seasons of reaching the NFC Championship Game. With Owens now out wide, the sky was the limit. While many Philly fans expected big things, I don't think anyone anticipated the impact that Terrell Owens was about to have on the franchise in 2004.

In his debut game, Owens pulled down three touchdowns. Through the first ten games of the year, he led all NFL players with 13 receiving touchdowns. After a December win over the Washington Redskins, the Eagles, poised to make a Super Bowl run, led the NFC with a record of 12–1.

However, the next week, against the rival Dallas Cowboys, Owens sustained his first major injury. After being ripped down on a horse-collar tackle by Cowboys safety Roy Williams, Owens was in pain. He refused to get on the medical cart. Instead, T.O. limped off the field and headed toward the bench. After the game, the medical results were in. Owens had severely sprained his ankle and fractured his fibula. The injury would require surgery, which included the insertion of a screw into his leg. T.O.'s season appeared to be over.

Philadelphia finished the regular season at 13–3, earning a first-round bye in the 2004 NFL Playoffs. With Owens on the sidelines, they defeated the Minnesota Vikings in the NFC Divisional Round and took down the Atlanta Falcons in the NFC Championship Game a week later. Philadelphia was headed to their first Super Bowl since 1980.

Although they stayed afloat without Owens, it was clear that Philly would be overmatched without their star receiver against the New England Patriots in Super Bowl XXXIX. The Patriots had won two of the previous three Super Bowls and lost only two games during the 2004 season.

Despite being on one leg and receiving disheartening information from doctors who said he wouldn't be able to walk in time for the gridiron showdown, Owens made sure he would not miss the big game. "Anything is possible if you keep faith in Him," Owens told me. With his faith in God, the use of Microcurrent, and a hyperbaric chamber, Owens was ready to go. Since the doctors did not clear him to play, he was forced to sign a medical waver to release the Eagles of any liability. In a Boston.com article, Dr. William Morgan of St. Elizabeth's Medical Center said, "He could suffer a career-ending injury if someone hits him in a certain way below the knee."

Many would not even dare to attempt what Terrell was about to do, but that's what separates Owens from the herd. He was built for these types of moments. All that time grinding alone in the weight room at college. All that time running sprints outside his grandma's house. All that time spent down on the courts in the gyms of Oakland. Owens was a driven warrior who sacrificed too much to miss this.

Although Philadelphia ultimately fell short in the game, Owens played out of his mind. On one leg, the receiver defied the odds and caught nine passes for 122 yards. To this day, it is one of the most memorable performances in Super Bowl history.

In 2008, as a member of the Dallas Cowboys, Owens became the first player in NFL history, age thirty-five or older, to have a 1,000-yard, 10-touchdown season. Only Jerry Rice has more 1,000-yard, 10-touchdown seasons than the kid from Alexander City. Owens would finish his career with six Pro Bowl selections and five first-team All-Pros. He currently ranks third all-time in receiving touchdowns, third in receiving yards, and seventh in career receptions. In 2018, to cap off his illustrious and sensational career, Owens was voted into the Pro Football Hall of Fame, the highest honor for any former player. Not bad for someone who didn't start on his high school football team until his senior year.

Terrell Owens finished his NFL career with eight seasons of at least 1,000 receiving yards and 10 touchdowns. The only other player in NFL history with more seasons is Owens's former teammate, Jerry Rice.

When I talked to Terrell about success, not just on the football field, but life in general, he used an analogy that I believe is beneficial for all of us. "I always equate it to a bank account. You only get out of it what you put in. Putting in the work is you making deposits into your account." Owens later mentioned, "You just gotta work on it. It doesn't happen overnight." Wise words from the quiet, reserved, boy from Alexander City.

Self-driven people are the ones who are first in the gym and last to leave. They are constantly outworking the competition and are overly focused on their mission. Even if they haven't yet reached the heights they set out for, they look at themselves as great. Self-driven individuals are willing to learn from others who will help them get to the next step. When life throws them a curveball, their drive keeps them going.

You see, it's not enough to just be motivated. There has to be something deep down that truly drives you. If you are having trouble identifying what this could be, ask yourself a simple question: "Why did I get up this morning?" While this may seem odd, really give it thought. By the way, saying "because I had to go to work/school" does not cut it. I want an in-depth reason as to what made you put two feet on the floor when you could have easily just laid in bed.

Once you confidently come up with an appropriate answer, try and analyze yourself for a week. Jot down mental notes in your head of what you found interesting throughout the day. When you had down time, how did you utilize it? What types of information did you consume? What kind of music did you enjoy listening to? What ideas recirculated throughout your head on a daily basis? Having a clear understanding of your hobbies and activities that you enjoy is an easy way to not only get to know yourself but also to truly find out what it is you hope to attain.

If you're still searching for answers, ask yourself another basic question. "How do I want to be remembered in one hundred years?" Once you identify why you got up and what you want the world to remember you for, you become that much closer to understanding what you want out of this life.

In college, Terrell knew that he wanted to be a professional football player. In order for that goal to come true, he was forced to run the extra mile, spend more time in the film room, and get extra reps in the gym while others were home resting. While all of this seems like a lot, Owens's drive to be great at football kept him from stopping. Once you find out what drives you, the work becomes easier, and you will never have to worry about going through the motions.

So how can we accurately become more driven? Science tells us that the place of origin for our motivation comes from the nucleus accumbens. The nucleus accumbens is the department where neurotransmitters release chemical messages to other parts of our body. In terms of motivation, the most vital neurotransmitter is dopamine, one of the more than a hundred neurotransmitters in our brain. According to John Salamone, PhD, the head of the Behavioral Neuroscience Division at the University of Connecticut, "Dopamine helps bridge what scientists call psychological distance. Say you're sitting at home on your couch in your pajamas thinking you really should exercise, for example. Dopamine is what enables you to make the decision to be active."

For motivation to truly kick in, the dopamine must take the mesolimbic pathway, a pathway that lies within the striatum and ventromedial prefrontal cortex.

To further harp on the value of dopamine, scientists from Vanderbilt University performed a brain imaging study, comparing "go-getters" and "slackers."

According to Vanderbilt University's website, the researchers found that "go-getters," who are willing to work hard for rewards, had higher release of the neurotransmitter dopamine in areas of the brain known to play an important role in reward and motivation: the striatum and ventromedial prefrontal cortex. On the other hand, "slackers," who are less willing to work hard for a reward, had high dopamine levels in another brain area that plays a role in emotion and risk perception: the anterior insula.

While it can act in opposite ways depending on where it is stored in the brain, dopamine has been proven to impact our drive. A lack of dopamine is commonly linked with a shortage of motivation and focus, fatigue, insomnia, and moodiness. BrainMD highlights eating foods rich in tyrosine (almonds, bananas, avocados, eggs, beans, fish, chicken), exercising regularly, meditating, getting the proper amount of sleep, receiving a massage, listening to music, or taking a supplement as the seven most effective ways to boost dopamine.

So, really get to know yourself. Find out who you truly are and what you want out of this life. Take the necessary steps to increase your dopamine levels, and once you hit your stride, keep going!

Paramount Points

- You get out what you put in, so *get up and get after it.*

- Know exactly where and who you want to be, and don't stop until you get to the top of that mountain.

- Do not get discouraged if you are not where you want to be in life. If you make it a point to get up every day and work hard, eventually, your time will come.

- Only you know what you are truly capable of. Never let your present status deter you from hunting those dreams.

CHAPTER FOUR

Eat Right, Exercise, and Watch Your Swagger Rise

The story of professional golf could not be told without Gary Player. Player, a South African-born athlete, is widely credited for bringing fitness to the sport in a way no one had ever imagined.

Growing up, Player was invested in sports like cricket, rugby, soccer, and diving. However, his father's infatuation with golf led Player to shift his focus to the green. His dad, Harry, took him as a fourteen-year-old to a local course for his first round of golf. Believe it or not, Player made par on his first three holes. From then on, he was hooked. "I started practicing daily," Player said. He told me he "would even skip school to practice my bunker play or to hit a few putts."

The more Player concentrated on golf, the more he realized this sport would not punish his body as much as sports like rugby, where one can be tackled at any moment.

Before heading off to fight with the Americans and British in WWII, his older brother, Ian, who saw great potential in Player, provided the teen with a significant dose of advice. "Gary, you're small, but if you promise me you will exercise every day, it will give you a chance to accomplish your dream," Ian said.

"It's a promise I have adhered to for nearly eighty years since," Player told me.

At seventeen, Player informed his father he wanted to be a professional golfer. He said, "I told him that the world would be my university, through golf and travel." Although he disagreed with his son's decision, Player's father trusted the teen, sensing that there was something special in him. Player found out later in life that Harry took out a bank loan to buy his son his first set of clubs.

In order to turn his dream into a reality, Player knew he would have to sacrifice much of his time. "My mentality was to work harder than anyone else who was striving to become a professional golfer," Player said. "Golf is a lonely game. No doubt I lost out on a lot of fun activities with my family and friends."

Though it was abnormal to combine working out and playing golf, Player stayed true to his brother's words and made fitness a daily routine. "Running, lifting weights, stretching, meditation, yoga, you name it," Player said. "Anything to gain an edge." In the 1950s, fitness was considered detrimental to the body, especially when paired with golf. Critics claimed the physical toll that weight-lifting brought would have anyone out of the sport in a jiff. Player decided to test his luck, a decision that colossally paid off.

With all the time spent on the course and a little extra motivation with his future wife's father being a local pro, Player, after graduating from King Edward School and winning the Victor Ladorama, an accolade given to the best all-around sportsman, became a professional golfer at age seventeen. Two years later in 1955, Player won his first professional tournament, the Egyptian Match. The following year, Player won his first South African Open, something he would go on to win thirteen times in his professional career. Three years later, Player won the Open Championship at Muifield, his first major championship.

In 1961, twenty-five-year-old Player became the first international player to win the Masters, edging out Arnold Palmer by a stroke after Palmer's double-bogey on the last hole. "This fulfills a lifelong ambition for me," Player said in a 1961 issue of the *Democrat and Chronicle*. Now $25,000 richer,

Player continued winning, conquering the PGA Championship at Aronimink Golf Club in 1962. The fitness buff was now a US Open victory away from becoming the third golfer in history to win the Career Grand Slam (winning all four major championships: the Masters, the US Open, the Open, and the PGA Championship).

Player stayed grounded with all this success, knowing the glory would slowly fade if he took his foot off the gas. "If I needed to work on a shot out of the sand, ball striking or putting, I would spend as much time as I needed to feel comfortable," Player told me. He was even "sometimes hitting shots in the dark."

In order to join Ben Hogan and Gene Sarazen as the only golfers to claim all four major championships, Player, ahead of the 1965 US Open, headed off to Missouri a week early to train with Jack Nicklaus. Forgoing a PGA Tour event to prepare for the US Open would be one of the best decisions Player has ever made.

I asked Player about his mental preparation ahead of the big tournament. "I believe it was on the Wednesday [before] when I went up to the board and saw all the names of the past champions written in gold letters," Player said. "There was an empty spot at the bottom for 1965 where I visualized my name. Sure, I was athletic, but it was my mental belief that led me to trust that I could become a champion."

Staying mentally sharp, Player, in our talk, made sure to let me know that his physical routine didn't alter, no matter what was at stake. "The morning before the US Open, I was in the gym squatting 325," he said.

On June 21, 1965, Gary Player's name went up on the scoreboard. At age twenty-nine, Player defeated Australian golfer Kel Nagle in an eighteen-hole playoff and won the US Open. "When I started physical training, they laughed at me," Player told the *Reno Gazette-Journal* in 1965. "But after all, physical fitness won the American Open for me."

Even as he got older, Player stood by his dedication to fitness. In 1971, occupants in a Tokyo hotel were alarmed when they overheard loud, pounding noises. When the residents approached the corridor, they locked eyes with Player, who was minding his own business and getting a little cardiovascular workout in.

That same year, the *Lowell Sun* published a piece on Player in which he described his workout routine. He would get to the gym by six thirty in the morning five days a week and run at least two miles a day. This drastically improved his golf game. "I have increased my average drive by 15 yards in the last ten years," Player said. Hoping to open the eyes of the readers, Player harped on just how important health and fitness really are to the human body. He said, "Obesity is responsible for more illness and death than anything else. In 1937, there are statistics showing the cost of medical care to be $4 billion in America. In 1968, it was $54 billion. Obviously, it has increased since then."

With regards to mental tension, Player said, "Exercise or physical action is prescribed as the best solution. It is far better than taking a drink or cigarette every time you have a little tension." Player understood something in the '70s many of us still don't understand.

In 1995, *The Tampa Bay Times* summed up Player's legacy perfectly, stating, "While Arnold Palmer could be seen smoking a cigarette on the golf course, and Jack Nicklaus carried his 'Fat

Jack' moniker, Player lifted weights, did sit-ups, and tried to condition his body to the demands of the game."

Fast-forward to 2009, and there was Player, out on the Augusta green, competing in his fifty-second Masters, the record for most tournament appearances.

In his career, which lasted over six decades, Player won nine major championships and a total of 167 professional tournaments. He is undoubtedly one of the greatest golfers to walk this planet.

As a pioneer in bringing fitness to the green, Player is the main reason why the Major Tours now have traveling gymnasiums available to the players at all times. Exercise between rounds, something that the athletes use to scoff at, is now the norm for anyone looking to succeed in the sport. A quote from an article in the *Orlando Sentinel* describes Player's influence: "If it weren't for trendsetters such as Player, who was squatting 300 pounds forty-five years ago while others laughed, golf still might be lost in the cigar smoke that clouded clubhouses and the players lounged in them."

"So to sum it up, how did staying active and eating right give you that edge over the field?" I asked Player.

"Think about this. You're competing in a major championship in the blistering heat and humidity. Miles of walking and probably thousands of balls hit. You look over at your opponent—he's out of breath and sweating profusely," Player told me. "But you've trained your body and mind for this exact situation. I'm oozing with confidence and have more in the tank than when the tournament started."

Only five golfers in the history of the sport have been able to win all four major championships during their career (PGA, The Open, US Open, Masters): Jack Nicklaus, Tiger Woods, Ben Hogan, Gene Sarazen, and Gary Player.

At eighty-three, Player is the same weight he has been for the last sixty years. Sticking to his Mediterranean diet of organic meat and fish and plenty of fruits, vegetables, nuts, and whole grains, Player stays away from processed foods and sugar, emphasizing that "sugar is really poison."

To stay active, Player continues to play golf, and he keeps his schedule jam-packed. "I am a working man. Always have been and always will be," he said. "I love to be on the farm with my horses and get my hands dirty or [be] in the garden planting trees. Rest is rust!"

Sticking to a routine filled with physical exercise and healthy eating has benefited Player far beyond the sport of golf. He said, "Humans are creatures of habit, and the daily, weekly, monthly routine you establish can set yourself up for success. Setting goals and the process to achieve them is very important, whether in sport, business, marriage, or everyday life." By the way, numerous research studies have shown that routinely working out has shown to enhance our memory and overall brain function.

As a parent of six, Player leads by example. "There are so many things in life that are out of one's control. Taking care of your body through a proper diet and exercise program is something you can," he said. "And in turn, this gives you energy to accomplish more. Your health is your most important attribute—mental and physical."

Gary Player is a perfect example of how a healthy body also leads to a healthy mind. "I always make sure my schedule allows for time to exercise," he said. "What I have done as I have aged is to train my mind that my body can still move fast. I set the treadmill to the fastest setting and sprint for ten to fifteen minutes. Some people assume they must slow down to prevent injury while it's the contrary. Just keep moving." Remember, this man is in his eighties and is still working out harder than most Americans ever will.

Player ended the interview with a heavy dose of inspiration. He said, "A person's most valuable assets are their health and time. Regular exercise and a proper diet ensure better health and likely more quality time on this Earth. Smile. Be happy, Present yourself well, Travel. Be positive. Have enthusiasm, and never stop learning."

Thank you, Mr. Player, for showing us what eating right and physical exercise can do. Below are a few tips to get you going in the right direction.

As far as the diet goes, the broad recommendation is to cut out as much sugar as possible and avoid processed foods. Today, according to Harvard Medical School, 66 percent of US adults and 33 percent of our nation's children are deemed overweight or obese.

In 2011, *Harvard Health Publishing* presented a "Healthy Eating Plate," which was a plan to educate Americans on what foods to nourish themselves with. The plate put a heavy emphasis on the importance of vegetables and fruits while also emphasizing whole grains like oatmeal, whole wheat bread, and brown rice as opposed to refined grains, which serve as sugar in our bodies and have been shown to elevate the chance of heart disease and type 2 diabetes.

A diet rich in healthy proteins such as poultry, fish, beans, or nuts is highly advocated for. If you plan on consuming meat, please make sure that it is pasture-raised. Pasture-raised meat is extremely nutritious, and contains no hormones, antibiotics, GMOs, or glyphosate. The same principle goes with fish. Always make sure your poultry is wild-caught, and not farm-raised.

Also, if you decide to eat out, be very mindful of the food you put into your body. When eating out at restaurants, you are more prone to be exposed to harmful PFAS chemicals. PFAS chemicals can be detrimental to our health, as science has found that exposure to these chemicals can be associated with liver damage, thyroid disease, obesity, hormone suppression, high cholesterol, and even cancer.

In 2019, Researchers at the Silent Spring Institute studied data from over 10,000 individuals in the National Health and Nutrition Examination Survey. Participants were asked about what they ate over the past twenty-four hours, week, month, and year. In doing so, the individuals also allowed their blood samples to be analyzed for specific PFAS chemicals.

Following the analysis, researchers concluded that "people who ate more meals at home had significantly lower levels of PFAS in their bodies. The vast majority (90 percent) of these meals consisted of food purchased at a grocery store. In contrast, people who consumed more fast food or ate more frequently at restaurants, including pizza places, tended to have higher levels of PFAS in their bodies." Unless you know all the ingredients in your meal and where these ingredients come from, just stay home and eat.

In a recent study, researchers gathered information on more than 70,000 individuals' diets, specifically examining plant protein intake. The research team compared those who consumed the most plant protein to those who consumed little to none. According to the *New York Times*, those whose diets were rich in foods like spinach, broccoli, and legumes had a 27 percent lower rate of cardiovascular death and a 28 percent lower rate of death from heart disease.

The study also concluded that a high intake of plant protein may help you live longer. The group who ate the most plant-based proteins boasted a 13 percent lower mortality rate than the individuals who consumed the fewest amount of greens and beans. Eat your vegetables people.

When it comes to cooking oils, stick with plant oils like olive or canola. These fats drastically lower cholesterol and have shown to be great for the heart. Avoid too much butter and trans fat.

For hydration, stay with water, tea, or coffee. Obviously, choosing a glass of water over a sweetened beverage will help you limit your calorie intake from liquids, which will aid you in controlling your weight.

In 2019, two thousand Americans took part in a research study conducted by OnePoll. These individuals were asked to reveal how many glasses of water they drank per day and were then requested to rate their overall happiness levels. The statistics displayed that 80 percent of individuals who drank over ten glasses of water per day deemed themselves as "very happy." Among those who claimed to drink four or fewer glasses of water per day, only 45 percent claimed to be "very happy." Overall, 67 percent of the individuals who felt like they drank "more than enough" water reported to be "very happy." Among those who acknowledged that they didn't consume enough H2O, only 21 percent of them rated themselves as "very happy." Those who drank a lot of water were three times more likely to achieve more happiness than those who don't absorb enough.

In that same year, thirty-six adults gathered together to take part in a research study conducted by Feng Lei, assistant professor at the NUS Yong Loo Lin School of Medicine's Department of Psychological Medicine. Feng and his colleagues assembled the subjects into two groups: people who regularly drank tea and non-tea drinkers. After three years of evaluation, the research team concluded that habitual tea drinkers had superior, more orderly brain regions than those who did not consume it. In his prior studies, Feng also noted that adults who consistently drink tea lower their chance of cognitive decline by a whopping 50 percent.

As far as coffee goes, the number one piece of advice is to avoid going over the daily recommended intake. When used properly, coffee can give you superpowers. Caffeine, the primary ingredient in coffee, serves as a stimulant by energizing our central nervous system. This natural compound has been proven to boost our alertness and amplify our focus. According to the University of Michigan Health Service, humans can sense the effects of caffeine within just fifteen minutes of ingestion, and the revitalizing upshot can last up to six hours.

Stanford University researchers followed one hundred people over a handful of years and concluded that those who persistently drank coffee tended to live longer than those who did not. A Spanish study in which 20,000 people were observed and, on average, followed up with after ten years, further backed-up the previous statement and found those who consume four cups of coffee a day actually lessened their chance of death by 64 percent compared to non-coffee drinkers.

If you're going to consume alcohol, please limit your intake. In an article published on Science.com, researchers profiled a study with mice to see if alcohol intake had any sort of correlation with cancer. When the body consumes alcohol, it is immediately transferred into an extremely toxic substance known as acetaldehyde. This studied carcinogen permanently harms the DNA within our blood stem cells. Any sort of DNA damage can lead to cancer. Not only could you potentially increase your odds of a cancer diagnosis, but you are also causing oxidative stress when you throw back some liquor. Oxidative stress can weaken an individual's ability to absorb nutrients. Did I mention it is terrible for your liver, brain, heart, and overall well-being? A drink or two a week has been shown to be fine, but please don't consume more.

The food we eat can positively or negatively alter our mood, depending on the choices we make. In Harvard Health Publishing's "Nutritional psychiatry: Your brain on food," Doctor Eva Selhub writes, "Eating high-quality foods that contain lots of vitamins, minerals and antioxidants nourishes the brain and protects it from oxidative stress. If substances from 'low premium' fuel [what you get from processed or refined foods] get to the brain, it has a little ability to get rid of them. Fueling up with processed or refined foods will also elevate inflammation and oxidative stress levels." The publication goes on to mention other studies that found a direct association between a diet rich in refined sugars and impaired brain function. The more refined sugars we consume, the more likely we are to suffer from mood disorders like depression.

95 percent of our serotonin, which according to Harvard Health Publishing is "a neurotransmitter that helps regulate sleep and appetite, mediate moods, and inhibit pain," is manufactured in our gastrointestinal tract, which is lined with millions of neurons, thus making sense that the inner workings of our

digestive system do a lot more than just help us digest food. These nerve cells truly conduct our emotions.

In 2011, Michael Berk, a professor of psychiatry at the Deakin University School of Medicine in Australia, conducted a study with his peers comparing the effects of a Western-type diet, made up of processed and fast foods, and a diet consisting of meat, fruits, and vegetables. The study included more than five thousand adults. The study concluded that those with a high intake of processed, low-quality foods were far more likely to be depressed and suffer from anxiety disorders than those with a polished diet made up of good proteins and vegetables.

The same is true for anxiety, and spinach is one of the best foods to eat to alleviate that anxiety. According to an article published by Harvard Health Publishing, other great nutritional options to relieve anxiety include foods rich in zinc (oysters, cashews, liver, beef, and egg yolks), Omega-3 fatty acids (wild Alaskan salmon), and Vitamin B (avocados and almonds). Eating pickles, sauerkraut, and kefir, three probiotic-rich food options, have also shown to lower social anxiety symptoms.

Additional findings concluded that anxious feelings appear to coincide with a lowered total antioxidant state. With that said, foods high in antioxidants (beans, fruits, berries, nuts, and vegetables) will help reduce stress and anxiety.

The more active we are, the less stress we will have. According to the Anxiety and Depression Association of America, scientists concluded that consistent aerobic exercise (walking, dancing, running, swimming, etc.), will not only help you sleep better and boost your self-esteem, but also help you control your moods and lessen your overall levels of tension. Just five minutes of aerobic exercise will spark anti-anxiety effects.

Even a little bit of exercise a week can do wonders to our body and overall well-being. Neuroscientists at the Oregon Health and Science University studied a group of mice to determine how a small burst of exercise can affect the brain. The scientists gathered a handful of mice and observed the rodents as they hopped on a running wheel and ran a few kilometers for short periods, over a span of two hours. Following their workout, the research team concluded a small amount of exercise boosted the function of Mtss1L, which led to an increased connection between neurons in the hippocampus (the region of the brain associated with learning and memory). Even a short workout (of four thousand steps), will legitimately make us smarter.

If all that science confused you, let me put it in basic terms. The better you eat, the better your mood will be. The more sugar, refined grains, and processed foods you consume, the more likely you will suffer in a handful of ways. The more we exercise, the better physical shape we will be in, and the better off our minds will be.

For those who struggle with their sugar intake, listen up. If you cut out processed sugar, the natural sugars in fruit and vegetables will eventually taste just like candy. In a recent interview, Dr. Michael Greger, an American physician, author, and professional speaker, said that once we cut sugar from our diet, our taste buds will immediately begin to evolve. "The ripest peach in the world will taste sour after a bowl of Fruit Loops," Greger said. On the other hand, once you go a week without the junk food, biting into an apple or eating a sweet potato will taste amazing.

A study published in *The American Journal of Clinical Nutrition* further emphasized Greger's stance. Researchers followed adult-aged men and women for five months and divided the participants into two groups. For three months, Group A followed a low-sugar diet with a clear mandate to replace simple sugars with proteins, fats, and complex carbohydrates. Group B did not alter their sugar intake. Every month, the participants were asked to judge the sweetness strength and their overall preference for various vanilla puddings and raspberry beverages.

After the first month, the researchers saw no differences between the two groups. In the second month, Group A assessed the low-sucrose pudding samples as more intense than Group B did. During month three, Group A judged both the low and high sugar concentrations in the vanilla puddings as 40 percent sweeter than Group B. Altering our sugar consumption directly effects how we perceive the sweetness of food and drinks.

I asked Gary Player if he had any personal experience with this idea. He told me, "Absolutely. No question since I have cut my sugar, fat, and salt intake, my taste buds changed dramatically. For example, I no longer take milk or sugar with my tea or coffee and can now actually tell the difference between [tea and coffee] brands."

So do yourself a favor by hitting the gym and avoiding sugar and processed foods. I always recommend eating as if you were preparing to hang out with a caveman, hundreds and hundreds of years ago. This means eating the foods that come from this Earth—all of the "one ingredient" foods like fruit, vegetables, nuts, whole grains, poultry, and fish. Health is wealth.

Paramount Points

- Eat *healthy foods*.

- What we put into our bodies has a *major* effect on our overall well-being.

- Make physical exercise a priority in your life.

- Not only does a little exercise help us physically, working out has shown to have a positive impact on our brain and mood.

- Develop a routine. Both in the kitchen and the gym. Creating a plan will help you stay disciplined and locked-in on your body goals.

- *Health is wealth.*

Chapter Five

Performing under Pressure

Humans are born to run. Our muscles, tendons, and bones have unique adaptations that other primates simply do not possess. In 2004, Carl Zimmer, a decorated science writer, blogger, columnist, and journalist, published an article in *Science Magazine*. In his write-up, Zimmer refers to research by University of Utah biomechanics expert Dennis Bramble and Harvard physical anthropologist Daniel Lieberman. The pair of scientists performed an experiment in which they put both humans and other apes on treadmills to further investigate anatomical traits. The two concluded that the nuchal ligament, a ligament located in the back of our necks, serves as an elastic band which has evolved over time in all animals considered "runners." Scientists believe that this particular ligament helps keep a runner's head from bouncing back and forth.

Lieberman and Bramble also found that tendons in our legs serve as springs, which "store about half of the energy of each stride and release it in the following one." The ordering of tendons in Chimpanzee's legs differ drastically.

And what about our rear ends? In the piece, Zimmer states, "By attaching electrodes to the gluteus maximus muscles of very cooperative volunteers, they [Lieberman and Bramble] have found that these muscles contract during each running stride, but not during walking—probably to stabilize the trunk." On the flip side, chimps have petite behinds.

Based off indications in our fossil records, it is believed that these distinctive adaptations for distance runners came together about two million years ago—long before humans had created any sort of hunting weapon. Before the bow and arrow, Homo, one of the early genus, were scavengers who used stone tools to break bones and cut meat from other animals' carcasses. "If you get [to the carcass] before the hyenas and the other hominids, you would have a lot of protein and fat at your disposal," said Lieberman. In order to get the most nutritional value out of their food consumption and fight off other species, our early genus had to move fast.

In 776 BC, the first-ever foot race took place at the original Olympic Games. Just about three hundred years later, legend has it that Pheidippides, a Greek soldier, sprinted nearly twenty-five miles from Marathon to Athens. The Greeks had defeated the Persians at the Battle of Marathon, and Pheidippides was chosen to give this message to the people of Athens. Not exactly built for this type of cardio workout, Pheidippides allegedly collapsed and died shortly after spreading the news.

At the first international Olympic Games in 1896, the coordinators of the event acknowledged Pheidippides by creating a 24.85-mile race. The "marathon," as they called it, was hosted in Athens, and stretched from Marathon Bridge to Olympic Stadium.

More than a century later, Deena Kastor won the 2006 Flora London Marathon with a time of 2:19:36, which is still the US record for the women's marathon event. Three weeks before that, Kastor won the 2006 Berlin half-marathon in an American record of 1:07 while breaking the ten-mile record of 51:31. At the 2005 LaSalle Bank Shamrock Shuffle in Chicago, an 8k road race, Kastor set both a World and US record, winning the event with a time of 24:36.

At the 2004 Summer Olympics in Athens (no pressure), Kastor won the bronze medal in the marathon event and became the first US woman since Joan Benoit in 1984 to earn an Olympic marathon medal. The year prior, Kastor set the US record in the women's 15k road race at the 2003 Gate River Run in Jacksonville.

Prior to competing at the professional level, Kastor attended the University of Arkansas, where she earned a degree in writing and ran track. During her time as a Razorback, Kastor won seven individual Southeastern Conference (SEC) titles. At Agoura High School in Agoura Hills, California, Deena won three state D-1 cross-country titles and a pair of state 3,200-meter track titles.

So how exactly has Kastor been able to sustain this unimaginable run of success under the hardships and adversity of competing at the highest level? Was she always immune to the pressure, or was this a mindset she developed over time? I spoke with the legendary distance runner to find out.

"I was in middle school when it was very clear I wouldn't become a better soccer player, nor could we find a position on the softball field to hold my attention," Kastor said. "I was too skinny to be graceful in ice skating, or so the instructor told my mom. The local track club welcomed everyone. I could jump, throw, sprint, or run, but I seemed to be placed with the small-distance running crew for the sake of building my self-esteem, the mission of my mom at the time." At age eleven, despite starting being somewhat ostracized in other sports, Kastor had found a pastime that she would dedicate over thirty-five years to.

Although she wasn't Mia Hamm on the soccer field, Kastor immediately excelled in track. The more Kastor put one foot in front of the other, the greater her passion for running grew. "Running gives you everything and anything you need. If you are social and need quiet time to collect your own thoughts, running is a good choice," she said. "We know running is good for our heart health, lungs, to develop muscle tone, and to build bone strength to offset osteoporosis. What is more important is the benefit to our mental health. Running releases feel-good hormones in your body, and, in doing so, cortisol, a stress hormone, is lowered. If we work on our positivity, we get a boost to these effects."

Again, Kastor enjoyed a myriad amount of success at both the high school and collegiate level, but it wasn't until turning pro that she hit her stride. In order to put herself in the best position for success at the top level, Kastor moved to the high-altitude town of Alamosa, Colorado. When sprinting at high altitudes, you increase your chances of becoming dehydrated, since oxygen levels decrease the higher you go up in altitude. At eight thousand feet, Alamosa is the ideal altitude for long-distance runners. Excelling under harsh conditions puts you in the position for greater success when the circumstances aren't as bitter, which is exactly why Kastor chose to train in Alamosa.

The harder she trained, the more her confidence grew. As we know, when physical preparation converges with mental tenacity, an athlete can accomplish a lot. More winning means higher expectations, which ultimately puts more pressure on that individual.

However, pressure can be tamed with the proper outlook. When asked about how she dealt with the bar constantly being raised the more she was victorious, Kastor noted that she "didn't think of it as pressure but as support. [I'd think,] 'Wow, the media believes in me. Cool, other racers are going to let me control the race.' If there was negative pressure from naysayers, I would graciously show them I could defend my title—that in fact, it wasn't a fluke. Pressure allows us to focus on a single task and take care of all the little things that will allow it to come to fruition."

Our perception is everything. So, if we approach a high-pressure situation with the proper attitude, anything is possible. Kastor could easily feel overwhelmed before competing against 40,000 individuals who want to outrun her. Instead, she embraces the high-pressure situation. "I like to set high goals because it makes me hunker down and train hard, recover hard, eat an abundance of nutrient-rich foods, go to bed early, soak myself in belief, simplify my schedule, and take care of my body," she told me. "Even if I don't reach my goal, I was a far better athlete for striving high."

One of the most memorable times when Kastor reached her goal was the marathon event at the 2004 Summer Olympics in Athens. Ahead of the colossal event, Kastor worked on her technique with male runners. While training, Kastor donned heavy, long-sleeve shirts to mimic the sweltering weather she would ultimately face on the track from Marathon to Panathinaiko Stadium. Not only did Kastor's physical preparation help alleviate pressure, but she also provided herself with a better understanding of the task at hand.

While most would be unwilling to go through the rigorous training that comes with performing at the highest level, Kastor never let being burnt-out or mentally drained stop her from working toward glory. "When you have lofty goals, your desire to get out and progress toward them is usually high," she said. "That being said, fatigue can turn anyone into choosing to sleep in over getting after it again. That's when I take the next step. Just make coffee. Just put on your shoes. Just open the door and get out. Just run to the next street. Then, you're out, so you might as well keep going!"

With this positive mindset, Kastor was locked-in. After weeks of strenuous practice, the night before the monumental competition was finally upon her. "So what is going through your head when you are less than twenty-four hours away from pushing your body to the extreme?" I asked. Kastor responded by noting, "The night before a big race, I always look at my training log. I'm not sure why doubt seems to creep in the week leading up to a race, but I have a training log to silence it. I flip through the weeks of highlighted good workouts, of smiley faces and little stories in the margins." The long-distance runner went on to state, "I see weekly numbers like 140 miles, but sometimes I see 70 and know I needed a rest day or two. Even that number shows me my body asked for rest, and we gave it what it needed. Simply skimming the pages usually puts a smile on my face."

Kastor's method is echoed in research. In a study by Gerardo Ramirez and Sian L. Beilock, students were asked to jot down their thoughts and emotions for ten minutes prior to testing. When compared to a previous test in which the students had sat quietly without writing their thoughts and emotions, those who wrote for ten minutes before the test received higher scores.

After reflecting, Kastor kicks it into high gear. "I think of three reasons why I should succeed in the race. It might be because I had the best mile repeat session of my career two weeks earlier, or it might be that my family is there to support me," she said. "Just as we nourish our bodies with good food, we need to nourish our minds with positive thoughts." Take full control of the situation by projecting positive results. The power of the mind is significant. Believing in yourself keeps your mind from creating any unsettling thoughts.

On August 22, 2004, eighty-two competitors from forty-six nations stood at the starting line in Marathon, Greece, all aiming to cross that finish line before anyone else.

As she gets ready to toe the line, Kastor heightens her focus and own the moment. We can fully mentally and physically prepare, but if we aren't locked-in when the time comes, we will underperform.

When asked about her secrets to "getting in the zone," Kastor replied, "I take a deep breath and calmly demand that I make the best of this moment. That's all I can do. Whether training went fantastically or it was heavily flawed, my job in that very moment is to be the smartest, toughest, [most] resilient, and committed runner I've worked myself to be. With all the months and miles of training, I owe it to my coach, team, and myself to deliver the best of me right up until the finish line. When we can do that, no matter the outcome of the race, we can be proud of the performance and keep hungry for the next one."

Five kilometers into the women's marathon at the Games of the XXVIII Olympiad, Kastor stood in twenty-eighth place. Despite the slow start, Kastor didn't wobble. She had a plan in the moment, which separates good from great and average from legendary. "Racing a marathon is very task-focused," she told me. "I get on pace for the first couple miles, assess how I am feeling, and hope I am determining at these early stages that I feel fantastic. I focus on getting fluids every five kilometers, staying on pace every mile, and lining myself up for any course tangent coming up. Every now and then, my thoughts are interrupted by the smell of chocolate chip cookies or a spectator holding a funny sign, but mostly I'm reading the course, checking my watch, and taking my fluids."

About six miles into the race, Kastor had crawled up to seventeenth place. By the midway point, she sat in twelfth. "The real work happens between mile eighteen and twenty-two, when I have to begin negotiating, pep-talking, and willing myself another mile," she explained. "But the moments when things get hard are when we have the chance to push through to greater heights."

Forty kilometers in, Kastor had skyrocketed into fourth place but was still 18 seconds behind Ethiopia's Elfenesh Alemu, who was positioned to win bronze. Despite the separation, Kastor persisted. "In most cases, the hardest races are the ones I'm most proud of and the ones that certainly built my character a little more persistent, a lot tougher, and more resilient."

With under a mile left from the finish line at Panathinaiko Stadium. Kastor glided by Alemu and ultimately finished 55 seconds ahead of the Ethiopian runner. "When I entered the stadium, I didn't know if I was in fourth or third," Kastor told the *Los Angeles Times* in 2004. "When I heard the announcers say third, I burst into tears. I couldn't control myself. With the course and the history, it's all just wonderful." It had been twenty years since the United States had earned a marathon medal, but Deena Kastor was locked-in and refused to disappoint.

Kastor credits her incredible run of success, no pun intended, to her willingness to always improve. She said, "The longevity of my career is due to understanding why it gives me joy. I never focused on wins and money as benchmarks of happiness or success. I relish in the pursuit of progress. And now in my forties, when progress doesn't come from seeing faster times on my watch, I am caught in the game of positive thinking."

Kastor went on to state, "running has developed an optimist in me that has positively affected my entire life. I never want that part of me to atrophy. Being human, I've had lulls in training, plateaus both mental and physical. When this happens, I immediately return to what gives me the greatest running pleasure—exploring. I venture to a new trailhead and explore new scenery. This always rejuvenates my running spirit. For others, it may be getting a new pair of running shoes, asking a friend or family member to join them, changing the time of day you get out, or refreshing the songs on your running playlist. Our individual job is to know why we want to stick to a plan, what makes us tick and keep going. Persistence is one of the greatest virtues in any success story."

What makes Kastor's insight on pressure so beneficial is that it is applicable to every task we take on, not just running a marathon. At the end of our conversation, Kastor opened up about dealing with the pressures that life bestows on us and how she avoids falling into anxiety in a high-stakes situation. The star athlete referenced her academic days, stating, "I did terribly on the SAT because of this. I overthought all the questions instead of using the knowledge I had. Preparation is the best remedy, but if you find yourself ridden with anxiety in the face of a challenge, try putting it in perspective."

She concluded our chat with four different ways to approach common high-stress scenarios. Number one, "give yourself the advice you would give your friend or sister. [Tell yourself], 'it's just a driving test. The worst-case scenario is that Mom will still have to drop me off at school. Or maybe I can have a friend take me.' or, 'This performance will give me a benchmark to grow from.' "

Secondly, meditate. "Try a three-minute meditation ahead of time to get out of the cycle of anxiety and quiet your mind," she said. "I love the *Headspace* app and do it with my daughter some days after school."

Her third piece of advice: put your energy and focus toward how you will act after you succeed! Whether it's a math test in school, applying to college, taking a driver's test, or competing in a sport, set aside time to mentally project how you will react when you achieve your goal. Maybe you'll celebrate with your family after scoring the winning goal or maybe you'll grab ice cream with your friends after acing that exam. Whatever the objective is, map out how you will behave when you are triumphant. "This shows your subconscious that there is, in fact, a good life after this stress," Kastor said.

Lastly, *dream big*. "Take the hypothetical in a positive direction. I mean if we're going to think ridiculously, let's have more fun," she said. "What if I master this driving test and impress the instructor so much that he gives me the keys to his BMW convertible as a gift? What if I play Jingle Bells so well that they move me to violin's first chair and I get recruited by the Boston Philharmonic?"

No US woman has ever finished a marathon with a better time than Deena Kastor's incredible mark of 2:19:36 at the 2006 Flora London Marathon.

In 2014, Mustafa Sarkar of Nottingham Trent University and David Fletcher of Loughborough University directed a study, "Psychological resilience in sport performers: A review of stressors and protective factors." Sarkar and Fletcher studied thirteen individuals with careers in sports, business, politics, and entertainment. The two polled the participants about various topics, including how they dealt with stress and a list of examples in which they overcame adversity in their professions. Sarkar and Fletcher documented the answers and highlighted the similarities that led to each individual succeeding under pressure. One major constant happened to be resilience. The ability and decision to never give up. No matter what.

Other keys to dealing with pressure, according to Sarkar and Fletcher's findings, included a positive outlook, a sense of control, being able to adapt, recognition of social support, and having balance and perspective on the situation. Remember, no matter how big a test may seem or how colossal a sporting event may appear, avoid overthinking. If you don't get the outcome you hoped for, note the necessary changes you need to make, and keep moving forward. If you do achieve your aspirations, give yourself a pat on the back, and keep moving forward.

When asked by the *Los Angeles Times* what it was like to accomplish such a historic feat in Athens, Kastor responded by saying, "The second I crossed the finish line, I was already thinking about preparing for [the New York Marathon]." No matter how remarkable the achievement may be, the greats in this world always put one foot in front of the other and continue to progress.

Paramount Points

- The best way to combat the emotional toll that comes along with pressure is mental and physical preparation.

- Whether they are positive or negative, acknowledge all of your emotions ahead of a big event.

- Prior to a high-pressure situation, you'll always feel like you needed more time to prepare, and that's okay. Control what you can control, and trust that the groundwork you laid was enough for success.

- The night before you find yourself in a high-stakes circumstance, take deep breaths, practice meditation, project positive outcomes, and *dream big*.

- If you don't get the outcome you hoped for, note the necessary changes you need to make and keep moving forward. If you do achieve your aspirations, give yourself a pat on the back and keep moving forward.

CHAPTER SIX

Don't Be Afraid to Fail

*"You have to go through a little adversity to realize
your potential."*

November 4, 2001. After a commanding 15–2 victory in
game six, the Arizona Diamondbacks, in just their fourth
year of existence, were one win shy of their first World Series
Championship. That year, the Fall Classic was somewhat of a
David vs. Goliath matchup. In the opposing dugout stood the
men in grey and blue. The New York Yankees were looking
to hoist the Commissioner's Trophy for the fourth straight
season, and, late in the game, it appeared as though they just
might do it.

Curt Schilling had started the Game seven showdown for
Arizona and was cruising right along. Heading into the eighth,
Schilling had allowed just one run and struck out eight batters.
Unfortunately for Arizona, New York Yankees pitcher Roger
Clemens was equally dominant. The American League's Cy
Young Award winner that season, Clemens struck out ten
Arizona batters and allowed only one run before he was
replaced in the seventh inning.

With the game tied 1–1 in the eighth inning, New York Yankees
budding star Alfonso Soriano took a called first strike. The
following pitch, Schilling got Soriano to swing and miss on
a ball in the dirt. As the rain continued to drizzle down in
Phoenix, Soriano managed to foul off the next two pitches.

Hoping to finally get him out, Schilling threw a pitch down
in the zone, that, unfortunately for him and the entire
Diamondbacks nation, was timed up perfectly by Soriano. The
twenty-five-year-old second basemen sent the ball about fifteen
rows back in the left-field bleachers. Yankees lead, 2–1.

Arizona had gotten out of the inning without allowing another run, which meant they were one swing away from tying the game. Although they had just six outs left, there was still life in the Diamondbacks' dugout.

However, right on cue was number 42. New York Yankees closer Mariano Rivera was on in relief, hoping to close the door on any comeback. For anyone unfamiliar with Rivera, he is arguably the most dominant relief pitcher to walk this planet. The Fox telecast flashed a graphic across the screen as Rivera warmed up that showed his career postseason ERA of 0.70 with the words "BEST ALL-TIME."

Rivera struck out the first two batters of the inning before allowing a single to the Diamondbacks' Steve Finley. The hit by Finley ended up doing no harm, as Rivera struck out Arizona's Danny Bautista on three pitches. Randy Johnson retired the Yankees in order the following inning, and Rivera trotted back on the mound in hopes of ending Arizona's magical season. At this point, according to *Baseball Reference*, Arizona had just a 22 percent chance of winning the game.

Yet, in this winner-take-all game seven battle, the start to the inning was unusual for Rivera. He allowed a leadoff single to Mark Grace. There was life for Arizona. Almost 50,000 were in attendance at Bank One Park, all on their feet. The next batter bunted the ball back to the mound, but an inaccurate throw by Rivera allowed both men to base. Men on first and second, nobody out. Arizona was just 180 feet away from tying this one up.

Hoping to get a runner to third, the Diamondbacks chose to bunt again, but this time, Rivera made a clean throw and got the force-out at third base. With men again on first and second, the Diamondbacks were down to their last two outs. Next,

Arizona shortstop Tony Womack was up at the plate. Among all the Arizona primary starters that year, Womack had the worst on-base percentage of the bunch. However, as you'll soon find out, statistics can be very misleading.

Womack lined a Rivera pitch into the right-field corner, allowing the man on second to make it home. From being four strikes away from defeat, the Diamondbacks had tied the game, and with men now on second and third, the pressure was on New York. Craig Counsell, the next batter up for Arizona, was hit by a pitch which loaded up the bases. Luis Gonzalez, Arizona's best hitter, slowly strolled up to the plate.

It had been a magical 2001 for Gonzalez, who really took his career to the next level when he was traded to Arizona in 1998. During his first year with the Diamondbacks, "Gonzo" hit .336 with 26 home runs, both career highs. He was selected to his first All-Star team and even earned a few MVP votes.

Gonzalez started out his wizardly 2001 campaign by clubbing a National League record of 13 home runs in April alone. In a June game against the Kansas City Royals, Gonzalez tied a franchise record when he hit 3 home runs in one game. The following month, Luis defeated Sammy Sosa in the championship round to win the Home Run Derby. He would finish the season with 198 hits, 36 doubles, a career-best .429 on-base percentage, and a franchise-record 57 home runs. To put his miraculous year into perspective, the only other player to get that many hits, doubles, home runs, and have that high of an on-base percentage all in the same season was Babe Ruth, who accomplished this feat eighty years earlier in 1921.

Fast-forward to October, and Gonzalez has the chance of a lifetime. As a kid, one can only dream of this scenario. A hit or a fly ball deep enough for the runner to tag up on, and Gonzalez goes down a legend in Arizona.

In spite of that, New York wasn't scared. Especially with Rivera on the mound, who had dominated Gonzalez in the past. As a member of the Detroit Tigers in 1998, Gonzalez faced Rivera on two separate occasions: he grounded out to second base the first time and hit a lazy pop-up to the shortstop the second.

In the 2001 World Series, Gonzalez was 0 for 3 against "The Sandman." He struck out looking on four pitches in game three, grounded out to the first basemen in game four, and struck out swinging the inning before this pivotal plate appearance. Every time he had faced Rivera, Gonzalez had failed to do his job.

When I asked Luis what made Rivera so difficult to hit, his answer was pretty simple. That famous cutter he threw was "like a Pac-Man. It just kept coming in and getting you on the handle every time."

Remember *Pac-Man*? That video game where you control the yellow Pac-Man character and attempt to collect all the dots before the four multi-colored ghosts get to you? I was never good at it, but I understood that if you compared a baseball to that little yellow figure that flew around the board, it meant the hitter was probably in trouble.

"So Luis, you struck out the inning prior and have never had any success against this guy. What's going through your mind as you step in the box?" I asked the five-time All-Star.

"You don't think about the past," Gonzalez said. "You gotta put that behind you and worry about the present. You put the past at-bats behind you." While the past plate experiences had not led to the outcome Gonzalez had strived for, he still stood confident. "You need to put the negative behind you and focus on trying to be positive," he said.

Gonzalez took a big hack on the first pitch, fouling it away. Down 0–1 in the count, Gonzalez asked the home plate umpire for time. He stepped out of the box and took a deep breath. Although he was hitless against Rivera up to this point in his career, Gonzo was ready for the moment.

In all honesty, he had been ready for this moment since he was a kid. Luis grew up in Tampa, Florida, a predominantly Cuban community. At the local coffee shop, a group of Cuban gentlemen would all sit together, play dominoes, sip coffee, and read the newspaper. The primary substance of their conversations always circulated around the Tampa-born baseball players who had made it to the big leagues.

As a child, Luis would head off to the shop with his grandparents or parents to get Cuban bread and coffee. He would hear the men talking about what the Tampa-born players did in the games the night before. It was at that moment that Luis knew he wanted to be professional baseball player. "I wanted to be the next guy they talk about," he told me. "When they opened that paper, I wanted them to read about Luis Gonzalez."

When kids were home relaxing or out with friends on their time off from school, Luis begged his family to take him to the batting cages. It was his passion. Baseball was everything to him.

Gonzalez, now back in the batter's box, stood confidently in his open stance. Steve Finley, Gonzalez's teammate at the time, said that "It was so loud, you couldn't hear yourself think." Luckily for Luis, big crowds were nothing new. Gonzalez grew up playing Little League ball with Tino Martinez, the New York Yankees first basemen at the time. Their Little League rival, Tampa's Belmont Heights team, also had a pair of eventual big-leaguers, Gary Sheffield and Derek Bell. When these two squads squared off, thousands of people would watch the twelve- and thirteen-year-olds play.

Rivera came to a set and the pitch. Joe Buck called the game in the booth: "Floater, center field, the Diamondbacks are World Champions!"

Fall five times, get up six. Luis Gonzalez's bloop single into left-center field gave the Arizona Diamondbacks their first World Series Championship in franchise history.

History of Gonzalez Facing Rivera

Date	Game type	Outcome
4/24/1998	Regular season	Groundout to second base
4/25/1998	Regular season	Pop-out to shortstop
10/30/2001	World Series	Strikeout looking
10/31/2001	World Series	Groundout to first base
11/04/2001	World Series	Strikeout swinging
11/04/2001	World Series	Walk-off single to center field

In 2001, Luis Gonzalez finished the regular season with 57 home runs, 36 doubles, and a batting average of .325. The only other player to mirror those statistics in a single season was Babe Ruth in 1921.

High performers like Luis understand the importance of failing. It is vital to take time out of your day and do some research on a few of your idols or role models in life. You will quickly find that even the best of the best failed at some point. A recent study done at Colombia University revealed that high school students' science grades actually increased after they learned that Albert Einstein and Marie Curie failed more times than they could even imagine. Students who were only taught about the achievements of Einstein and Curie saw their grades go down.

Makes sense right? When you learn about someone's failures or mishaps, you humanize them no matter who they are or what they have accomplished. Anything relatable can be seen as a connection. If Einstein failed numerous times, yet was still incredibly successful, then I can also be successful no matter how many times I fall down.

The value of failure cannot be determined in an equation. Failure can only be understood through experience. As humans, we all have times where things don't go as planned.

The beauty of life is we can always keep trying. If you don't succeed on the first try, that doesn't mean you are destined for eternal failure. Think of Gonzalez. Before that at-bat, he had failed all five times against Mariano Rivera. Do you think that stopped him from getting in the batter's box for a sixth time?

Absolutely not.

Some people will succeed faster than others. It may take you longer to learn how to ride your bike than your neighbor. You may fail your driving test or take longer to graduate college than the average student, but that is totally fine. Heck, even failing as infants is alright.

A recent study showed that early walkers are not more advanced or intelligent than those who spend a little bit more time on all fours. When you graduate from college, it doesn't matter if it took you four years or forty years. Everybody receives the same diploma. If you fail your driving test three times before passing, you get the same license as someone who passed the test with flying colors on the first attempt. Success comes at different times for different people. Those who experience more success in life are the individuals who get back up when they fall down.

The act of evaluating a past experience—breaking down what you did right and what you need work on—has been shown to do wonders. In 2007, Shmuel Ellis of Tel Aviv University conducted an experiment involving two companies of soldiers in the Israel Defense Forces. These groups were tested on their completion in navigation exercises. According to *Harvard Business Review*, following standard military practice, Company A endured a series of after-event reviews in which they concentrated solely on the mistakes they made on that particular navigation assignment. Company B broke down what could be learned from not only their failures but also their successes. This experiment went on for four days.

Two months later, the pair of groups went through two more days of navigation exercises. Two conclusions were drawn. First, those who zeroed in on both success and failures actually learned at higher rates than the soldiers who focused solely on failing. The second finding illustrated Company B soldiers also appeared to learn faster because they had evolved "richer mental models" by evaluating their experience from both a positive and negative perspective. Evaluating your past experiences from every angle leads to more success.

From 1993 to 2004, Joseph Loscalzo, MD, PhD, Brigham and Women's Hospital Harvard Medical School, evaluated fifty illustrative compounds with an intent to measure the success and failure rates of each drug. After his experiment, he concluded that four out of five drugs failed when entering phase II testing.

In 2013, Major League Baseball players on average got a hit just 25.3 percent of the time. In an article published on Weather Spark, researchers analyzed the success rate of meteorologists in San Francisco over a three-month span in 2011. Following the study, it was noted that these "weather-predictors" had "an overall error rate for predicting precipitation over three days of 15 percent, with precipitation predicted but not observed 43 percent of the time, and precipitation observed but not predicted 10 percent of the time."

The goal of this story is for readers to understand success habits in the simplest way possible. Successful people do not quit until they reach their goal. When you feel like you have failed, break down exactly why the experience played out how it did. Look yourself in the mirror and think about what you can do differently in the future so that the past does not replay itself.

It's very simple: when you fail, keep going. That's really it. If you make a promise to yourself that you will never give up, you will eventually succeed.

Besides bringing us closer to success, failure provides us with valuable experiences we would not receive had we not put ourselves in a success/failure situation. I am sure you are familiar with the phrase, "You miss 100 percent of the shots you don't take." If you are too scared to talk to someone, too scared to apply for a job, or too scared to take a test, you'll never know what you are truly capable of in life. That is why you need to get out there and shoot. Shoot until your arms fall off.

Paramount Points

- Don't be afraid to *fail*. We learn more from failure that we do from success.

- Failure just means you are a step closer to success.

- Avoid thinking about your past failures, as it does no good. In general, dwelling on the past is toxic, but worrying about past disappointments is deadly.

- When you come up short, jot down why you failed and what you learned from the experience. This will help you next time, as you will know exactly what to avoid and recall what worked.

- Once you succeed, people will forget about all the times you failed, so keep going after it!

- Failing is part of life. Next time you fail, understand that your shortcoming makes your story that much more epic.

CHAPTER SEVEN

Develop Your Passions

As an infant, Ryan Sheckler loved to climb. Whether it was stairs or sofa cushions, the California-born kid had a knack for getting on all fours and scrambling up anything he could find.

Before he was two years old, he decided he also enjoyed spending time on a skateboard. "I was literally on the board at eighteen months," he told me, reminiscing about the time he found his father's skateboard in the garage.

When Ryan was five, his dad, Randy Sheckler, gifted his son with his very own skateboard. To make the board stand out, Randy added custom grip tape that created a "sunset-like" design and caught Ryan's attention. "That was the first moment where I saw the creativity you could have with skateboarding," he said.

Soon after, he started to hang out with the other neighborhood kids, who also shared a love for skateboarding. Randy built the pack of boys a multitude of ramps, and off they went. "We would all skate every day. *Every day*," he emphasized. "That was the only thing I wanted to do."

While wearing his pinstripe helmet with "gnarly flames," Sheckler slowly started to acquire a talent for the sport. "I picked it up fast because I liked going fast," he said.

The majority of the neighborhood clan was four to five years older than Ryan, so the young boy knew he would have to work extra hard to fit in with the "big kids." One day, as he watched the other boys performing kick flips off the curb and other stylish tricks, Sheckler rushed home to his parents and said, "I wanna be like the older kids. I wanna do those cool tricks." With a goal on his mind, Sheckler, along with help from Mom and Dad, derived a plan of doing one hundred kick flips a day. While the exercise was rather monotonous, the young skater's desire to be great kept him from losing focus. "I did one hundred a day because I wanted to," Sheckler said. "I was fully dedicated as a little kid to the craft of skateboarding because it was so intriguing to me. I had such a passion for it."

Pretending to be Tony Hawk, Christian Hosoi, Steve Caballero, and John Cardiel, Ryan practiced and practiced some more. For his sixth birthday, the Shecklers actually invited Tony Hawk to hang out with Ryan and his friends at the YMCA Skate park in Encinitas, California. To much amazement, the megastar informed the family that as long as he received five hundred dollars and some chocolate cake, he was game. "That was his appearance fee," Sheckler laughed. "That's how real and OG he is."

With boarding the only thing on his mind, Sheckler quickly surpassed his peers in his south Orange County neighborhood. At age seven, Sheckler entered his first skate contest for seven- to ten-year-old skaters. Ahead of the event, he felt uneasy. "I felt nerves for the first time," he said. "I cried before the contest." It was in this moment that Randy Sheckler knew his son would be a champion. "He could see I wanted it. He told me, "nerves mean you want it."

Possessing a mix of emotions, Sheckler won his very first skateboarding contest. From that point on, he was addicted to the feeling of victory. "After that, I kept skating every day. I was in contests every other weekend," he said.

The more victorious he was, the faster he climbed. At nine years old, Sheckler was already competing against teenagers in factory-sponsored contests. Despite the age disadvantage, Sheckler won a handful of events, which caught the eyes of professional skateboarder Rodney Mullen.

At thirteen, Sheckler received a call on the family house phone. The mysterious caller, who claimed to be Mullen, was interested in speaking with the child prodigy. Assuming it was a prank call, Randy informed the star to "F-off," and slammed the phone down. Luckily for Ryan and the entire Sheckler family, Mullen called back and insisted he was no phony. After Randy was finally convinced, Ryan hopped on the phone, and the rest is history. Sheckler agreed to sign with Mullen's skateboard company, Almost Skateboards.

Now a professional, the teen was immediately eligible to compete in the 2003 Summer X Games in his home state of California. In his only park event at the competition, Ryan Sheckler became the youngest X Game gold medalist ever in Skateboard Park. In Sheckler's first round, the rising eighth grader earned 93.33 points and followed that up with a 93-point run, edging out Brazil's Rodi De Araujo, the defending tournament champ. Proceeding his epic showing, The *Los Angeles Times* published a 2003 article on Sheckler that that led off with "The future of skateboarding is five feet tall, ninety pounds, and wears braces." "It's rad," Sheckler said in the article. "I don't even know what to think. I seriously had no intentions of winning. I just came out to have fun and just skate with the guys I've looked up to all my life."

He followed up this performance by winning a gold medal at the Gravity Games and two Vans Triple Crown titles. On top of all this, Sheckler was even featured in a *Scooby-Doo* episode, playing himself. Four contests, four victories. "That's when I knew," he told me. "That's when I knew I'm put on this planet to skateboard and I'm gonna do it."

As his schedule started to get more hectic, Sheckler's parents pulled him out of his traditional school and started home-schooling him. The thirteen-year-old, who earned a six-figure income in his first year as a pro, had now taken his passion to a whole new level. Eight months out of the year he would travel to compete in a contest or film a skate video. During the few months that he was home, Sheckler hired a personal trainer who had him ride road bikes to keep his cardio up and legs strong.

While this may seem like a lot, Ryan was still that boy that loved to stay moving. Whether it was skating, "Racing motocross, go-karts, or surfing," Sheckler said, "I never stopped being active." He even spent time with Travis Pastrana, legendary motorsports competitor and stunt performer. Ryan, who refers to Pastrana as "the gnarliest dude alive," recalled a time when he was only twelve years old and hanging out with the modern-day Evel Knievel. "He put me on the front of the bike, and I was in charge of the brake and the shifter," he said. They rode around his supercross track. "He put me in situations that scared the crap out of me," Sheckler said. "But all of those experiences helped me really adapt to adrenaline and conquer my fears."

In 2008, at age eighteen, Sheckler won his second gold medal at the X Games by showing off some insane board slides, rotations, and flip tricks. By defeating Paul Rodriguez and Greg Lutzka, who placed second and third respectively, Sheckler had finally dominated a non-traditional park course as he flawlessly skated around the course outside of the Staples Center, that was built to duplicate a New York subway station. "This is the best thing I ever won, and the best I've ever felt," Sheckler said in a 2008 *Los Angeles Times* article. "It was the hardest I've ever skated, and I can honestly say all my hard work paid off."

After missing the 2009 street final because of a rolled ankle, Sheckler won his third gold medal at the X Games XVI in 2010. In the course that included a "teacup" feature, Sheckler performed an alley-oop frontside transfer from one half of the teacup to the other while showcasing a cab back lip and a frontside air on the teacup.

When I asked Ryan if he had any pre-skate rituals, the skateboard star informed me he is big into visualization. "I always had the ability to see myself doing what I wanted to accomplish. I would figure out what run I wanted to do, and then I would just sit down and close my eyes," Sheckler said. "I would go through the entire run, and I can see my board pop. I can see the way I lock into a trick and how I want my body to be." This in-depth visualization process allowed Sheckler to calm his mind and keep his heart from beating out of control. "Right before the run, I zone out and focus on my breathing," he said. "I take five deep breaths, crouch down, and I pray to Jesus."

Win or lose, Sheckler has been known to always sport a smile while competing. "I keep the smile on the whole time," Sheckler said. "Even If I fall, I keep the smile on because it's a passion, and it is such a blessing to be able to live my passion."

In 2003, Ryan Sheckler became the youngest X Games gold medalist ever in Skateboard Park.

I asked Ryan what he believes is necessary on anyone's path to greatness aside from working hard. The conversation quickly shifted to the importance of surrounding ourselves with positive people. "My inner circle is so powerful and full of love.

They want to see me happy," he told me. "It's the same way I want to see my whole circle of friends happy and prospering."

With a circle that includes his family, a pair of friends from kindergarten, and a handful of others he has met along the way, Sheckler has been able to flourish and overcome even the darkest of times. When he struggled with alcohol a few years back, his family and friends were there in full support. Sheckler credits the positive traits he possesses, being "loving, trustworthy, hardworking, creative, motivating," to those around him. By keeping positive friends and family around, Sheckler firmly believes, "we can do whatever we want to do if we have the right work ethic."

Ryan also serves as a role model to other skaters by spreading his positive energy and informing them of the overarching reason as to why we should be skating: "It's about being creative and progressing the sport that we love."

New York Times bestselling author Dan Buettner, who has studied healthy habits, backs up Sheckler's message. "I argue that the most powerful thing you can do to add healthy years is to curate your immediate social network," Buettner said in a *New York Times* piece. "Your group of friends are better than any drug or anti-aging supplement and will do more for you than just about anything."

Another vital part of Sheckler's journey has been his willingness to take risks. In 2007, Sheckler agreed to do an MTV show, *Life of Ryan*, a reality television series based on his daily life. Although he received backlash from the skateboard community, who believed Ryan was doing a disservice to the skater image by showing off a luxury lifestyle mixed with reality-TV drama, Sheckler used the opportunity to create a massive fan base. A fan base that he still has and that allowed him to create products and grow his personal brand. "Skateboarding is a finicky world," Sheckler said. "You're supposed to be dirty and not do your laundry. I was just trying to show the passion I had for this incredible sport to the world."

As we know, those who follow their passion in life are often the ones who inspire the most individuals. For Sheckler, following his lifelong passion gave him a true sense of purpose. "Skateboarding has made my purpose clear," Sheckler told me. "It's allowed me to know that what I am doing is inspiring people. It's inspiring kids to grab a board for the first time. This is what I'm here to do—show people the light and how creative you can be."

By following his true desires and dreams, Sheckler has added more value to this world than he ever imagined. In 2008, Ryan launched the Sheckler Foundation, which helps disabled children and injured and recovering athletes. Despite all the awards, money, and fame, the "gnarliest feeling you could ever have" according to Sheckler is skating with autistic children at his events. Parents of these autistic children watch as their children drop in on a ramp, with help from Ryan, and giggle for the first time as they experience the weightless feeling that skating brings. "The parents get emotional," Sheckler said. "They have never heard their kids laugh like that."

"So what do you say to the people who are too afraid to follow their passion and just settle for an everyday job?" I asked.

"How do you know it won't work? How do you know?" Sheckler said. "You have to give it an effort, man. There are so many times in the Bible where it says to 'never give up.' You cannot give up on your dreams."

Even during times of failure, Sheckler insists that sticking to your true hopes and desires is always the best option. "Where you prosper and where you find glory is trying something and then failing and trying it again" he said. "Maybe you fail ten times, but that's part of the desire and part of the passion." Sometimes, it takes Sheckler weeks to land certain tricks, but his love for the sport keeps him from quitting. "If you set a goal for yourself, you've got to at least follow it through until the end. Anything I can set my mind to, I can do."

In this internet age that consists of bullying and negativity, Sheckler encourages the youth to focus on themselves and weed out any negative energy. "We are all blessed in different ways," he told me. "You just have to find your calling. Figure out who you are, who you want to be, and what you want to stand for. Then, go after your goals. Go after them until the point of exhaustion. You have to give it 100 percent. You cannot settle."

The skater has broken both of his elbows and ankles on multiple occasions, suffered from a Lisfranc injury in his right foot, and has endured damage to both of his MCLs, but the twenty-nine-year-old wouldn't change a thing.

When I asked Ryan to summarize how skateboarding brings him excitement, the skater kept it real. "It's freedom for me," he said. "When I get on my skateboard, it's pure freedom. It's pure creative control. I get to do whatever I want to do." With a childlike sense of joy, Sheckler ended by stating, "Gosh, it's so fun."

Let's break down what following his passion has done for Ryan and his career. It's given him personal freedom, the ability to get out of his comfort zone, empowerment, an increase in self-confidence, a lust for life, immense career success, and, most importantly, a way to inspire and touch the lives of so many.

There is no reason why any of us should settle for a job that does not coincide with our true dreams and desires. You get one life. Why not do whatever it takes so that your occupation never feels like work?

Think about your relationships. The more you like someone, the more seriously you take that particular connection. Whether it is your partner, family member, or just a friend, if we feel a strong bond with another human, we automatically become more invested in that relationship. The same goes with jobs. The more passionate we are about a particular subject, the harder we will work in that field.

What you decide to do with your career will take up a good chunk of your time on this planet, so why not do what you love? It seems so simple, yet so many of us will just settle to get by. In order to truly know what we are capable of in life, we must follow our dreams!

If you are uncertain about what your true calling is, don't worry. Passions are developed over time. Pick a field that you find interesting, do some research on it, and see if it's a good fit. "If you look at something and think, 'that seems interesting, that could be an area I could make a contribution in,' you then invest yourself in it," said Gregory Walton, a psychologist at Stanford University who contributed to a university piece centered around passion. "You take some time to do it, you encounter challenges, over time you build that commitment."

As a kid, skateboarding was a major interest for Ryan. When he first started, he didn't even know what he was doing, but as time went on, he became more invested in it, was challenged in the sport, and eventually grew to obsess over it. Again, he developed this passion by dedicating his time to finding out if it was the right field for him or not. A good way to find out if a field or particular subject is best for you is by failing in that area. If we are passionate about something, we have a positive relationship with failure when we come up short in that desired field. Skaters who love to skate do not mind failing over and over since, at the end of the day, they are doing something they have grown to love.

So if acting is something you are interested in, join an acting class. If you would like to be a writer, start to write. Maybe you aspire to be a singer. Well, you better start singing. Passions are acquired, not fixed. Carry an open mind with you when you are trying something new. In Walton's paper, the authors said, "Those holding a growth theory should expect that pursuing even strong [passionate] interests will sometimes be difficult. If a fixed theory is associated with expectations that pursuing a strong interest will be easy, that belief may lead people to discount an interest if it becomes difficult." One of the other authors, Carol Dweck (Lewis and Virginia Eaton professor of psychology at Stanford) went on to mention, "It's the idea of broadening the possibility of having more interests, allowing for the possibility that your interests could stretch." Understand that there is always an adjustment period when you experience something new. Be open to new possibilities, and don't stop until you can confidently decide if what you are doing is a good fit or not.

From a scientific standpoint, developing harmonious passion in a particular field will lead to constant positive emotions which could not have been tapped into if one was not truly fond of that field. In *Psychology of Well-Being*, contributing author Robert J. Vallerand states that engagement with a harmonious passion is "hypothesized to lead to repeated positive affective experiences in the activity that spills over in one's life in general that, in turn, facilitates sustainable psychological well-being while preventing the experience of negative affect, psychological conflict, and ill-being." The more we stay open-minded and spend time doing what we have developed to enjoy, the happier we will be.

Paramount Points

- Developing your passions will undoubtedly drive you toward a fulfilling life.

- The only way to know if pursuing a career in something you are acutely passionate about will pay off is by getting up and trying!

- Blossoming your passions will open up doors for you that you could never imagine.

- If chasing a career that you are passionate about does not work out the first time, keep trying. We get one shot at life. We might as well follow our dreams and intuition.

- While on your path to victory, surround yourself with positive-energy individuals.

CHAPTER EIGHT

Be Confident

Passionate people are always the ones who emanate the most self-confidence. Passion brings us intensity, enthusiasm, and a little extra flare in whatever we are pursuing. At a young age, Mike Modano's love for hockey helped him spark not only an eventual Hall of Fame career in the NHL but also a self-confident mindset that he wakes up with every day.

Growing up in Highland Township, Michigan, Mike couldn't wait for the winters. Cold weather meant the lake that his family lived on would freeze over, allowing Modano to lace up his skates and work on his hockey skills. He said, "I was out there all day, every day. Before school, after school." And when it got dark, Modano said, "We streamed some lights up on the trees that were close to the lake." Even when Modano and his family moved off the lake and over to Westland, Michigan, Mike's mother, Karen, had a rink built in their backyard. With the easy ice access and sheer willingness to work on his craft, teenage Modano quickly became a household name.

At age fourteen, Modano made the Detroit Little Caesar's Midget Major team. Despite his teammates being two to three years older than him, Modano thrived, finishing with 66 goals and 131 points in 66 games for Little Caesar's. His exceptional play caught the eyes of Rick Wilson, general manager and head coach of the Western Hockey League's Price Albert Raiders. At first, the Raiders coaches were skeptical of the lanky teen from Michigan. In a 2007 *Los Angeles Times* article, Brad Tippett, Modano's former coach with the Raiders, said, "He came walking in, about six foot one and weighed about 145 pounds if he had about fifteen dollars' worth of quarters in his pockets. He had braces and bleached blond hair. We looked at each other and said, 'He's going to get killed.' "

However, the Raiders coaching staff quickly changed their minds when Modano first took to the ice for a tryout. "After about three minutes, we picked up our jaws and he was given the name 'Magic,' " Tippett said.

Despite his small size and the fact that he was only sixteen and competing with twenty-year-olds, Modano's confidence never wavered. "At a young age, there is a little bit of a no fear factor. The unknown doesn't really scare kids as it does adults as we get older," Modano said. "I was just out there having fun with the guys."

Modano went on to make the Raiders roster, and, in the WHL season opener on September 28, 1986, against the Brandon Wheat Kings, Modano notched three goals in Prince Albert's 8–2 victory. Not bad for someone who "could've passed for a thirteen-year-old," according to Wilson.

He went on to finish his first junior hockey season with 62 points in 70 games.

In 1987, now weighing around 175 pounds and receiving more ice time, Modano's stats skyrocketed. He ended the 1987–88 season with 127 points, including 47 goals in just 65 games. A few months after the season, Modano received a call that would change his life forever. Just four days before turning eighteen, the Minnesota North Stars selected Modano first overall in the 1988 NHL Entry Draft. Modano became the second American-born player to be drafted with the first pick, joining Brian Lawton, who was coincidentally also selected by the North Stars just five years earlier.

During his rookie year in 1989, Modano scored his first career goal and added an assist in the Stars' season opener against the New York Islanders. He then followed up that performance with a 2-goal game against the Hartford Whalers.

Despite the immediate prosperity, there were times when Modano struggled. He went eight straight games without scoring and was asked by reporters about the slump. Like any confident individual, Modano understood that it's not always rainbows and butterflies. In a 1990 article, he told the *St. Cloud Times*, "I've sorta gotten myself prepared for these sorta-slumps. They're gonna come my first couple years until I get some more consistency." Rather than beating himself up for not getting the results he wanted, Modano stayed calm and stuck to the plan.

At the end of his rookie season, Modano was named a member of the NHL All-Rookie Team, a squad made up of the best first-year players in the league. He led all teenagers with 75 points.

After four seasons in Minnesota, Modano nearly averaged one point per game, tallying up 309 points in 317 contests. Ahead of the 1993–94 season, the North Stars moved to Dallas and became the Dallas Stars. When I spoke with Modano, he said the change of scenery sparked his confidence and took his game to the next level. "How so?" I asked.

He said once the team moved to Texas, "I began to create a routine and pattern for how I handled my offseason." Outlining a twelve-week plan, which Modano said consisted of "Easy movements—simple stuff for the body the first four weeks" followed by "active movements the next four, and, last four, a lot of cardio, a lot of stuff on the ice, a lot of track work."

In one of our previous chapters, Gary Player spoke on the importance of a routine, but check this out. Over 91,000 adults in the United Kingdom took part in a study which was later published in *The Lancet Psychiatry* in 2018. The participants were asked to wear an accelerometer on their wrists to measure their daily activity levels. Daniel Smith, professor of psychiatry at the University of Glasgow, conducted this study with a team of researchers to observe the circadian rhythms (daily sleep-wake cycles) of adults in the UK and find out if a disruption in one's cycle had an effect on mental health.

After careful observations, the team concluded that those who had more circadian rhythm disruptions, meaning they were more active at night than they were during the day, were remarkably more likely to endure symptoms of bipolar disorder or depression. The researchers also noted that the more circadian rhythm disruptions, the more likely that individual's well-being would decrease.

Now, this is pretty obvious. Those who don't sleep well are going to suffer drastically in both a physical and mental way. We have known that for years, but this study is influential because it highlighted how a structured rhythm of being active during the day and dormant at night is crucial for your state of mind. All in all, if you wake up without a plan, there is a good chance your activity levels will be disrupted. Mapping out a routine for your day will force you to stay active and maintain a daily rhythm. If you do this while also sticking to a consistent sleeping schedule, you are setting yourself up for greatness and avoiding any possible mental disruptions.

Not only did his physical preparation help him boost his confidence, but the mental preparation was a big part in Modano making giant strides in his play.

A noted pre-game napper, Mike made sure to take at least a half-hour out of his day to mentally prepare for his next opponent on the ice. He said, "The mental side for me was a lot of visualization. Seeing yourself in a particular play or position on the ice." He went on to state, "Getting to see those plays over and over again in my head so that when it did happen, it was just instinctual. It was habit. It was automatic." Not only would he project positive outcomes occurring like making big shots or great passes, Modano would focus on people they were playing against. Breaking down the opposing goalie's strengths and weaknesses, he knew where he wanted to be and the types of shots he was looking to take later on that day.

That first year in Dallas, Mike Modano scored a career-high 50 goals at twenty-three years old. From 1994–98, Modano notched 345 points in just 316 games.

1998–99 was a special season for both Modano and the Dallas Stars franchise. In seventy-seven regular-season games, Modano led the team in goals (34), assists (47), and points (81). Dallas finished with the best record in the league, winning a franchise-high fifty-one games. In the first round of the playoffs, the Stars swept the Edmonton Oilers. In the Eastern Conference semi-finals, Dallas took down the St. Louis Blues in six games. One series win away from reaching the Stanley Cup Finals, Dallas was up against their toughest test: the Colorado Avalanche, led by Peter Forsberg and Joe Sakic. The two teams had squared off four times that season with the Stars only managing to win once.

When I spoke with Mike, I was curious if he approached "higher stakes" games different than the ones in the regular season. As we know, a test is different than a homework assignment, and a job interview has a lot more on the line than a conversation with a friend. However, Modano said his approach stayed the same. "Hone down your emotions and the mental side of it. Stay in your little bubble, do what you do.

Stick to your game plan, and know what to expect from your opponents," he said. Be aware of what's at stake, but don't change who you are.

After five games, the Avalanche held a 3–2 series lead over the Stars. However, Dallas claimed games six and seven to advance to the Stanley Cup Finals. In hopes of claiming their first Stanley Cup in franchise history, Dallas was slated to face the Buffalo Sabers, a team who was also seeking their first championship.

After a loss in game one, Dallas defeated Buffalo in game two, 4–2, to even up the series. Despite momentum shifting the Stars' way, Modano appeared to injure his wrist on the way to their victory. His left wrist was found to be broken. On top of this, SportsTicker claimed that Modano also separated his left shoulder. ESPN reported that Modano would be out the rest of the series, but the Dallas sniper had other plans.

Luckily for the Stars, Modano went on to suit up for the remainder of the finals, and, despite being physically injured, assisted on the Stars' final five goals of the series. Behind his incredible postseason play, leading all players in assists (18), Modano and the Stars hoisted the Stanley Cup Trophy, defeating Buffalo in six games.

In 2001, on an empty-net assist, Mike Modano became the Dallas Stars' all-time leading scorer. To this day, nobody in franchise history has more points than Modano. In twenty years with the Stars, he notched an incredible 1,359 points. His 561 career goals and 1,374 points are both records for American-born players. Since Modano entered the league in 1989, he is one of two players to have over 500 goals, over 800 assists, and a plus/minus over 100 (Jaromir Jagr being the other). In 2014, Modano was inducted into the Hockey Hall of

Fame. "I didn't wanna be a flash in the pan," Modano told me. "To be great was to be able to string together years and years of production and winning. Once you get a taste of winning, it becomes contagious. You don't wanna give up that feeling to anybody else."

Even with all his success at the professional level, Modano, like all of us, dealt with negative self-talk from time to time. "In hockey, there are a number of ups and downs," Modano said. "There are times when you fight those demons, but that's when you gotta go back to what got you there in the first place." When negative self-talk crept in, Modano made sure to stick to his foundation. "The knee jerk reaction is to get off and do something different, but that often makes it worse," he said.

Mike Modano's 561 career goals and 1,374 career points are the most ever by an American-born player in the NHL.

"So what are the keys to being a self-confident individual?" I asked.

"Controlling what you can control," Modano said. "In hockey, what gave me confidence was being in great shape, taking care of my body, mentally being prepared, and physically doing the right things in the offseason. Repetition is the mother of all skill."

Sure, most of us won't score over 500 goals in the NHL and lead a team to their first Stanley Cup in franchise history, but we all have the ability to approach life like Modano.

"I'm gonna play baseball on TV! I'm gonna play baseball on TV!" shouted six-year-old Andruw Jones as he ran around his house in Curaçao, a country located in the southern Caribbean Sea, about forty miles north of the Venezuelan coast. With an estimated population of less than 200,000, Curaçao is known mostly for its beautiful beaches and diverse culture. Since Curaçao has been under the rule of many different nations over its history, it is common for an islander to speak four languages. As a child, Andruw spoke Papiamentu and Dutch, while learning English and Spanish in grade school.

As a tourist, the colorful buildings located in the island's capital, Willemstad, are a must-see. These rainbow, shining buildings, located right on the water in the center of Willemstad, are the homes of many Dutch-style businesses. The old folktale goes that, originally, these buildings were draped in white stucco, which was tough on the eyes on a bright, sunny day. A local doctor at the time encouraged the city government to force these businesses to save the eyesight of the residents and paint their buildings. This suggestion ended up making vibrant architecture a part of the islands' identity.

Becoming one of the baseball players on TV was a pretty superb dream, especially since that goal really meant competing in the United States, a place where no Curaçao players had found any success. At this point, the only Curaçao-born player to appear in the MLB was Hensley Meulens, who hit just .220 in the show and never appeared in more than a hundred games in a season. It was also uncommon for any scouts to visit Curaçao and look for talent, making it even harder for guys to showcase their abilities.

Still, the fact that no Curaçao-born player had had any success in the MLB did not bother Andruw. He loved baseball, maybe even more than his mother's famous pork chops, which really says a lot.

When he wasn't in school, Andruw was playing baseball, basketball, or riding his BMX bike, except on Sunday, which was designated for family time and the beach.

At age eleven, Andruw was a budding star who played on a youth select team that traveled to Japan, Puerto Rico, and Venezuela to compete. When he was thirteen, a scout came to the island to watch one of his games. However, this man was really looking at one of Andruw's teammates. In this particular contest, going against fifteen-year-olds, Andruw sent a ball over four hundred feet for a no-doubter home run. The scout immediately turned his attention over to Jones, who was not even old enough to drive a car.

For the first time in the history of the Atlanta Braves, the storied franchise sent one of their professional scouts down to Curaçao to give Jones a private tryout. "I really didn't think about nothing. I was just happy to do what I wanted to do. I don't think about feeling nervous. Just go out there and make it happen," said Jones. "Go out there and have fun—everything will fall into place." Luckily for Jones, everything did fall into place. Paul Snyder, Atlanta's longtime amateur scouting director, watched in awe as Jones displayed incredible speed, elite defense, and an ability to crush the baseball. At just sixteen years old, Andruw Jones signed a $50,000 contract in July, 1993, to play for the Atlanta Braves. He packed his bags, said his goodbyes to family, and was off to the States for training camp the following February.

"How did you have this much confidence in yourself at such a young age?" I asked the former MLB star, who ended up crediting a lot of his immense confidence to his father.

"Growing up, he challenged me in a bunch of stuff, so that kind of built my confidence. [He would ask] 'How many push-ups can you do in a row? How high can you jump? How deep can you dive down there in the ocean?' " Jones went on to say, "If you're weak-minded, you're probably gonna have a hard time making it. You have to be hard-minded. You have to have one of those 'don't give a shit' type of minds so that you can succeed."

By being challenged in everything he did, Jones was able to develop a positive and poised mindset he carried with him for his entire career.

In 1995, his first full season of professional baseball, eighteen-year-old Andruw Jones excelled for the Class-A Macon Braves. He hit 25 home runs, knocked in 100 runs, and stole 56 bases. Because of his immense success, Jones was named Minor League Player of the Year.

The following season, Jones was promoted to high-A ball, where he tore it up for the Durham Bulls. In 86 games, Jones had a .313 batting average and belted 17 home runs. The Bulls were one of the best teams in the league and had clinched their division at the midway point in the season. The Braves front office had seen enough of Andruw at the A-Ball level and decided to promote him to AA, where he would suit up for the Greenville Braves.

The first two weeks were rough for Jones. He struggled with adjusting to the AA level and was hitting under .150. Still, the nineteen-year-old remained confident. "I'm not afraid of a failure. Because my failure is gonna make me better," Jones said. "If you are playing at a high level, you have the talent. Whatever scout, teacher, coaches that picked you to get there, they believe that you have the talent."

By remaining focused, confident, and being a little bit more patient at the plate, Jones raised his average to .369 and crushed 12 home runs in just 38 games. After his 17-game hit streak came to an end, Jones was off to the Richmond Braves, Atlanta's AAA ball club. The highest level before the Bigs. Jones was, by far, the youngest player on the Greenville team, a squad made up of players aged twenty-two to thirty-one.

Richmond ended up being a very short stay for the promising center fielder. Jones played in 12 games, and had 17 hits, including 5 home runs. He showed his ability to hit for average and power while covering all ground in the outfield and constantly swiping bags. After just 45 at-bats, Jones got the call. "Pack your stuff—you're going to the big leagues," his coach said. A six-year-old's dream had now come true.

The previous season, in 1995, the Atlanta Braves capped off their first World Series Championship since 1957, defeating the Cleveland Indians, four games to two. Poised for a repeat in '96, Atlanta had a dominant first half, winning 54 of their first 87 games. Jones, who was called up late in the season, appeared in 31 games and hit 5 home runs. Atlanta went on to win their division for the second straight season.

The Braves were able to sweep the Los Angeles Dodgers in the National League Division Series, but were challenged in the National League Championship Series by the St. Louis Cardinals. With the series tied at three games apiece, it was officially a must-win game. In the do-or-die game seven, Jones came up big for the Braves, going 2 for 4 with a home run and

3 RBI, helping the team blow past the Red Birds, 15–0. Atlanta was World Series bound for the second consecutive season and would square off against the New York Yankees.

After a rain-out postponed the start of the Fall Classic, game one of the 1996 World Series took place on October 20. Andy Pettitte, who won a league-high 21 games for the Yankees and finished as the runner-up in the AL Cy Young Award voting that season, got the start for New York. The teenage Jones was slated to hit seventh in the Atlanta batting order.

Pettitte had no problem getting through the first inning and started the second inning by getting Atlanta's Fred McGriff to strikeout swinging. The next batter was Javy Lopez, who got the Braves' first hit of the game, a single into centerfield.

With a runner on first, in stepped Jones for his first career World Series at-bat. Despite mild winds and a low temperature, Jones chose not to wear sleeves—an interesting move for "The Curaçao Kid," who was "just happy to be there." Jones stood confident in the box, knowing he was there for a reason. It was a challenge going up against one of the top pitchers in the game, but challenges were nothing new to Jones. Regardless of the lights and the 50,000 people watching, this trial was just like when his father would test him to see how many push-ups he could do. Nothing different, just stay focused, "continue what you're trying to do, and you will reach your goal," Jones said.

With the count at three balls and two strikes, Andruw Jones, the nineteen-year-old kid from Curaçao, became the youngest player in MLB history to hit a home run in a World Series game, a record that still stands today. To top it off, Jones, in his very next at-bat crushed a three-run home run to give the

Braves an 8–0 lead. He joined Gene Tenace as the only player to hit home runs in their first two World Series at-bats.

Only four players in MLB history have hit 400 home runs and collected at least 10 Gold Gloves: Ken Griffey Jr., Willie Mays, Mike Schmidt, and Andruw Jones.

Although the Braves ultimately lost the World Series, Jones proved he belonged on the team. For seventeen years, millions watched Andruw Jones play baseball on television, marveling at his extraordinary play. He was a five-time All-Star, and, from 1998 to 2007, was awarded ten Gold Glove Awards in a row. In 2005, the Braves superstar led the league with 51 home runs and 128 RBI. He finished runner-up to Albert Pujols for the NL MVP Award.

When it was time to hang up the cleats, Jones had 1,933 hits and 434 home runs. He is one of four players in the history of the sport to win ten Gold Glove Awards, while also hitting over 400 home runs. The other three are, Ken Griffey Jr., Willie Mays, and Mike Schmidt—three of the best to ever step foot on a diamond.

When I asked Jones how he was able to achieve such success, his response was simple: "I just wanted to become the best player that I could be." He went on to say, "I was confident in what I wanted to do my whole career."

Jones's and Modano's stories exhibit the roots of confidence from both ends of the spectrum. With Modano, we see confidence is attained through intense physical and mental preparation.

In a research study led by Michael Mrazek, psychological scientist of the University of California, Santa Barbara, and Jonathan Schooler, a psychologist and professor at the University of California, Santa Barbara, the two gathered forty-eight college students from their prestigious university. One group enrolled in a mindfulness class, while the others were appointed to a nutrition class.

Over the course of two weeks, the students in the mindfulness class learned about physical and mental methods to help them focus and stay present. Outside of the classroom, the students were advised to take part in some sort of mindfulness activity, whether that be some form of meditation, yoga, reciting positive affirmations, listening to music, or even coloring.

The kids in the nutrition class learned about the basics in nutrition science as well as ways to eat clean in the kitchen. When these students were away from school, they were asked to keep track of everything they ate but were not asked to change their diet.

After the two weeks, the students were tested again in the verbal reasoning section of the GRE and the working memory capacity exercise. The results showed that the students in the mindfulness course, who were not only taught ways to boost intelligence but also practiced on the side, had higher working capacity and better test scores on the GRE (a 16 percent improvement) than those in the nutrition class.

Setting aside time to not only learn about but also participate in mindfulness activities has shown to enhance your cognitive abilities. Whether you strive for a boost in memory, higher test scores, better physical performance, or just an overall advancement in your intellectual skills, taking some time out of your day to practice mindfulness is an extremely good idea.

Andruw Jones taught us being a self-confident individual is simply a decision. Yusuke Kinari of Kyushu University spearheaded a study on how confidence levels affect performance. In the experiment, participants were asked to solve a handful mazes. Ahead of the showdown, the individuals were divided into groups of four and were asked to predict where they would rank within their group, in terms of who would complete the most mazes in the allotted time.

When the researchers observed each individual, it was noted that those who displayed higher levels of confidence by ranking themselves more highly ultimately solved more mazes. The more confident you come across, the more productive you will be. If you go into a situation thinking you will excel, you are far more likely to succeed than if you enter that same scenario thinking that you will fail. Whether things go well or badly, you must just decide to be confident. Put the external context aside and make the choice to believe in yourself.

Confidence is not designated for some esoteric group. Those who are self-confident obtain this attitude through repetition, physical and mental preparation, and, most importantly, a never faltering mindset to trust that things will work out.

The key is to keep yourself honest. You know best what you are good at and what you need to work on. Practice doing things you need to improve on in the fields you wish to have more confidence in. Never focus on what others think, and don't spend any time wondering if you will succeed or fail. Just put in the time to find out what works and what areas you need to focus on to better prepare yourself for the future.

Paramount Points

- Before a big event, set aside time to mentally prepare for how you would like the affair to play out. A better understanding of what you are about to walk into will help you gain self-trust.

- Don't shy away from challenges. The more we put ourselves in success/failure situations, the closer we get to victory.

- The more reps we get, the more confident we will be in our desired field.

- Understand that you belong. Even if you struggle at times, never question your place in life.

- Having confidence is a decision, not some esoteric feeling for the elites. Just *decide* to be confident.

CHAPTER NINE

Make Sacrifices

The year is 1992. After a brief hiatus to earn a degree from Cornell Law School, Pablo Morales was back representing the red, white, and blue at the Olympic Games. Eight years prior, Morales won a relay gold and a pair of silver medals while swimming butterfly for the United States at the 1984 Summer Olympics.

In Rochester, New York, seven-year-old Ryan Lochte was glued to his TV, anxious to see how the twenty-seven-year-old Morales would fare as he prepared to compete in the 100-meter butterfly. Lochte, who was essentially raised around the swim deck (both of his parents were swim coaches) was infatuated with the sport.

BANG. The sound of the starting pistol went off, and the competitors dove into the pool like a set of dolphins, splashing on as they proceeded through the race.

Midway through, Morales and Poland's Rafał Szukała had distanced themselves from the pack, and it seemed it would be a photo finish.

As the two competitors touched the end of the pool, signaling they had completed the race, thousands of fans turned their heads toward the scoreboard, eager to see the final results. "SZUKALA: 53:35, MORALES: 53:32"

Swimming 0.03 seconds faster than the runner-up, Pablo Morales had just won his first individual gold medal. As Lochte jumped up and down in his living room, in awe of Morales's performance, he decided he was going to be a swimmer.

Not only was he wonderstruck by Morales's talent, but his character really drew Ryan in. "After he won, he congratulated all the other swimmers he raced against, and then I saw him get his towel and jacket and go around the pool deck to sign autographs and take pictures with fans. [I thought] 'I wanna be just like that guy.' That's when my aspirations of being an Olympian came about. At seven, I wanted to go to the Olympics, and I wanted to get a gold medal. I wanted to do that while breaking a world record. I set my goals really, really high," Lochte said in our conversation.

At age eleven, Lochte and his family, who were tired of the cold winters in New York, packed their bags and moved down to Florida. Instead of playing in the snow, Lochte would spend his free time riding the waves on the beach.

As a high schooler, Lochte played basketball and swam, but it was clear that his skills in the pool were astonishing for his age. As a sophomore at Spruce Creek, Lochte was named Boys Swimmer of the Year for his county. That year, Lochte finished the regular season with a record of 29–0 and won the 200- and 500-meter at both the district and Five Star Conference championships. In his route to victory, Lochte set school records in both events.

The next year, he was again listed as the top male swimmer in All-Central Florida, winning the individual Class 3A state championships in the 200- and 500-yard freestyle while also swimming on the 400 relay team that won the state title. "Most people get really focused for their meets. I just have fun," he said in a 2000 interview with the *Orlando Sentinel*. "I go in there, and I have a good time. I joke around, and I talk to my friends."

Following his prominent year, Lochte received full-time scholarship offers from a handful of the top collegiate swimming programs in the country. After his senior year, the four-time state champ chose the University of Florida to continue his education and help the Gators dominate in the water.

In January 2003, freshman swimmer Ryan Lochte was named SEC Athlete of the Week, after winning the 200-yard freestyle, and 200-yard butterfly in the Gators dual meet victory over SMU. Lochte followed this up by winning the 200-yard individual medley at the *Dallas Morning News* Classic. His time of 1:47.81 set a new meet record.

At the end of the season, Lochte, at eighteen, was named the SEC Male Swimmer of the Year. After one year, he ranked anywhere from first to seventh in school history for seven different swimming events.

In our conversation Lochte said, "After my freshman year, I said, 'You know what, I can make this into something big. I wanna go down in history as one of the best swimmers ever.' " Following his illustrious premier season, Lochte told me he became "locked-in" and started setting his goals even higher. "Every time I went to practice, I came with a purpose and something to strive for."

I was interested in seeing what kinds of sacrifices a Division I swimmer needed to make in order to reach the pinnacle of his profession. "I was waking up at five in the morning, going to swim practice, training for two hours and then, I was immediately going to breakfast, then going straight to my classes," Lochte said. "Classes were all day, up until afternoon practice, which consisted of more swimming." This swimming was then followed by an ab workout or some form of out-of-water training. "Then you can go home, eat, rest, and do it again the next day."

"What about a social life?" I asked. Ryan made time for friends but couldn't stay out too late, knowing he had to wake up at five o'clock each morning.

"Well, what about spring break? That must be a nice time to rest for the swimmers," I chimed in.

"When people go on spring break, you're staying at the college and training. The college is a ghost town, but those are the sacrifices you have to make in order to achieve the goals you want to accomplish."

In the summer, while most were on break, the Florida Gators swim team continued to take classes. While it wasn't a full course load, the training schedule was exactly the same. When I asked about sacrificing all this time, Lochte said, "The reward at the end is so worth it. I don't have any regrets of missing parties or anything like that. My schedule was waking up in the morning, going to swim practice, and trying to achieve my goals." Because of his hard work, dedication to the craft, and sacrifices, Lochte was given opportunities than many can only dream of.

In 2004, Ryan Lochte attended the US Olympic Team Trials in Long Beach, California. It was here he qualified for the team, finishing second to only Michael Phelps in the Men's 200M Individual Medley. After a fourth-place finish in the event final, Lochte also qualified for the 4×200-meter freestyle relay team.

That year, at the Summer Olympics in Athens, the Americans upset the defending champion Australians in the 4x200-meter freestyle relay. The quartet of Michael Phelps, Klete Keller, Peter Vanderkaay, and Lochte, who swam in the middle legs of the event, finished .13 seconds faster than the Australian team. "Once I step on those blocks, a switch happens in me where I'm no longer that laid-back Ryan Lochte, surfer from Daytona. I'm a racer. I'm a competitor," he said.

In Lochte's second event, the twenty-year-old won silver in the 200M individual medley.

Following the games, while most US Olympic athletes like Lebron James and Dwyane Wade, head back to the States with the money and immense fame, Lochte returned to Florida in preparation for the next two-a-day workout with his college team.

A few months later, at the 2004 FINA Short Course World Championships, Lochte won three more medals. He earned gold in the 4x200-meter freestyle with his three teammates, won the silver medal in the 200-meter individual medley, and bronze in the 200-meter freestyle.

The following year, Lochte won a pair of bronze medals, finishing third in both the 200-meter backstroke and 200-meter individual medley. Again, teaming up with Phelps, Vanderkaay, and Keller, the squad won gold in the 4x200-meter freestyle relay.

Two weeks after the 2006 NCAA Championships, Lochte, at the 2006 FINA Short Course World Championships in Shanghai, set new world records in both the 200-meter individual medley and the 200-meter backstroke.

Lochte earned his first individual gold medal at the 2007 World Aquatics Championship, winning the 200-meter backstroke over Aaron Peirsol, who had won the event the prior seven years. In his victory, Lochte broke Peirsol's world record.

When Lochte graduated from the University of Florida in 2007, he went down in history as one of the best SEC swimmers of all time. The half human, half fish, was named NCAA Swimmer of the Year twice, a seven-time SEC champion, and a twenty-four-time All-American.

Ahead of the 2008 Summer Olympics, Lochte spoke with the *New York Times* about his training habits. The article said, "Lochte swims three to five miles most days, sometimes even twice a day." and that to perfect his technique, he "tries to streamline underwater for at least 15 meters off each flip turn." In the gym, "three times a week for an hour and a half [to] two hours," Ryan uses free weights and machines to focus on building up strength in his shoulders, legs, and back. Ahead of his pool sessions, the article said, "Ryan does probably thirty to forty-five minutes of core body exercises three times a week."

Based off the sacrifices he has made, it should come as no surprise that Lochte won two gold and two bronze medals at the 2008 Summer Olympics in Beijing. Four years later, at the 2012 Olympic Games in London, he won five more medals, including gold in the 200M individual medley, an event that he had yet to win at the Olympics. At the 2016 Olympic Games, Lochte won his sixth gold medal as the United States edged out Great Britain and Japan in the 200-meter freestyle relay.

Ryan Lochte has earned twelve Olympic medals, making him the second-most decorated swimmer in Olympic history trailing only Michael Phelps.

As of right now, Lochte is the second-most decorated swimmer in Olympic history. He occupies the world record in both the 200-meter individual medley (long and short course) and 400-meter individual medley (short course).

I wanted to learn more about the psyche of an all-time swimming talent like Ryan. When I asked him about his mindset right before an Olympic event, Ryan said, "I don't have to think about my races because I've already done them so many times in practice that it's natural. It's like breathing. Repetition, over and over." As a competitor, Lochte said, "you need to be able to push your body harder than the people you're swimming against. I can empty the tank and keep going. I can outwork anyone. You know the other guy is just as tired as you are, but there's always another gear in you. You just have to dig deep down inside of you and pull it out."

As far as sacrifices go, Lochte told me, "You have to understand the sacrifices you need to make in order for something great to happen. When you achieve a goal, you won't even remember all the hard times you had. I don't even remember all the hard practices. You enjoy the moment once you get ahold of that goal. It's all about the journey. The journey is what got me there." Lochte sacrificed his time on a daily basis, which in turn, led to major personal success.

Nowadays, Lochte continues to make sacrifices in different ways. In 2017, Ryan's wife, Kayla Rae Lochte, gave birth to their son, Caiden Zane Lochte. Other swimmers that compete against Lochte are a lot younger and don't yet have families. After training in the morning, they go home, rest, and get massages. When Ryan goes home, he is a full-time dad and must dig deep down, just like he does as a swimmer, to find energy to play with Caiden. Having a son means a lot less rest and recovery, but Lochte was quick to mention that, having Caiden is "the greatest sacrifice I've ever made. I'm on cloud nine every day when I see my son."

While making sacrifices can be hard, the payoff is always worth it. Jörg Löschke of the University of Bern in Bern, Switzerland, published a section in the "International Journal of Philosophical Studies," in which he highlighted the value of making sacrifices. Löschke wrote, "sacrifices are difficult to make, and successful pursuit in difficult activities can also be intrinsically good." The pursuit of chasing a goal that requires major sacrifices will provide us with gratification once that feat is met.

Part of making sacrifices is giving up short-term happiness in order to enjoy a long bout of prosperity. Maxime Taquet et al., a multifaceted group of data scientists, physicians, and psychologists from around the globe, observed the moods and personal affairs of 30,000 people. By using a smartphone application, the team of intellects studied the individuals for about a month.

When the observations were complete, the group concluded that an individual's mood has a remarkable influence on the types of activities they partake in. They found that when someone is in a jolly mood, they are more likely to get involved with irksome, yet practical tasks like cleaning up around the house. On the flip side, when someone is feeling down, they tend to lean toward choosing affairs later on that day that are more delightful, like spending time with friends and engrossing in one of their hobbies. This, of course, is an effort to turn their mood around.

So why does this matter? Well, the data tells us that people are not always pursuing happiness-enhancing ventures. In fact, individuals only look for pleasurable affairs when they are in a bad mood, which further backs up the "hedonic flexibility hypothesis." Originally presented by American cognitive psychologist Herbert Simon, the hedonic flexibility hypothesis essentially states that humans have both short-term and long-term goals, and our mood helps us categorize these desires.

If you are in a bad mood, you are, as stated in the study, more likely to make an immediate change in order to bring instant happiness. On the other end, if you are like Clifford the Big Red Dog, who seems to always be in a cheerful frame of mind, you tend to think more long term and focus on your future. Successful and happy individuals are the ones who consistently give up their immediate happiness for long-term greatness.

In order to be great in any field, you must do what the majority of people are not willing to do. All high performers spend their time more wisely than the average human, which allows them to reach heights that most can only dream of.

If Ryan didn't dedicate a good chunk of his time to improving his swimming, there would be no gold medals. Whatever it is you want out of life, understand that in order to reach your goal, you will have to make sacrifices. Whether that be time with family, friends, or yourself, sacrifices must be made on your path to greatness.

Paramount Points

- In order to rise in this world, you must be willing to make sacrifices.

- Anyone who has ever achieved greatness has made an abundance of sacrifices along the way.

- While the sacrifices you make might feel like losses in the moment, there is no better feeling than accomplishing your long-term goals, especially after realizing what you gave up in order to reach something that many thought was not possible.

CHAPTER TEN

Positive Thinking Is a Superpower

Too short. Too skinny. Not physically built to last over the course of an entire MLB season. Tim Hudson has heard it all. While physical limitations can be disheartening to most, the former four-time All-Star never let his slight stature affect how he carried himself on the diamond.

Whether he was on the baseball field, basketball court, or throwing the pigskin around on the gridiron, Tim Hudson was always one of the smaller athletes on the playing field.

In elementary school, Tim would spend his free time with his two older brothers, Ronnie and Keith. By the time Tim turned eight, Ronnie and Keith had already graduated high school and were involved in a competitive softball league. Each weekend, the two older brothers would bring Tim along as they practiced for the upcoming tournaments. Since he was just a kid, Tim served as the ball shagger—the person who would retrieve the balls in the outfield after they were hit by the other players.

While it's obviously not the most glorious position, Tim looked at this unpleasant role in a positive light. He believed it helped build his arm strength, and being around older players gave him the opportunity to grow in many ways. In our conversation, Hudson said, "If you play with kids who are older than you, you have a tendency for your game to get elevated."

Not only did he believe spending time with his older brothers helped him develop as an athlete, Tim also credits his competitive fire to his big bros. In a 2001 interview with *USA Today*, Hudson said, "They never gave in. They always gave it everything they had. I saw how competitive they were and it just kind of rubbed off."

As a high schooler, Hudson was overlooked and didn't get the chance to pitch for the Glenwood High School baseball team until his junior year. During his senior season in 1993, Hudson led the Gators to the 1993 AISA state championship. He finished the year with a 9–0 record, 0.46 ERA, and 107 strikeouts, while also hitting .475 with 8 home runs and 16 stolen bases. Despite the elite statistics, no college program was interested in the undersized righty. He didn't throw terribly hard, topping out at around 85 m.p.h., and schools were not necessarily interested in offering a scholarship to a pitcher who weighed less than 150 pounds, no matter how gaudy his numbers were.

"I always felt like I was a bit of an underdog. I had that underdog mentality," Hudson said "Many people didn't know if I was going to be able to handle playing baseball at the next level, just because of my size. That was something that really motivated me when I was younger."

Rather than get discouraged, Hudson developed the "I'm gonna show you" mentality, which stuck with him throughout his entire baseball career. "If someone gives me a chance to play, I'm going to show them what I can do," he said.

Hudson was uncertain if his family would be able to send him off to college. In his mind, the choice was either get a scholarship to play ball or join the Air Force. Luckily for Hudson, B.R. Johnson, a baseball coach at a local community college, decided to give the outfielder/pitcher a shot. This gave Hudson the chance to stay local and continue playing the sport he loved. "Even though it was just one opportunity, it was the only opportunity I needed. All you need is just one chance. One person to believe in you."

While at Chattahoochee Valley Community College (CVCC), Tim worked his tail off, proving to himself and others that he belonged at the collegiate level. He was always one of the first guys at practice and one of the last to leave. Hudson grew an inch, gained about ten pounds, and quickly saw his velocity increase. In his first year, the freshman went 10–2 with a 2.45 ERA and piled up 107 strikeouts. From throwing in the mid-80s as a high school player, Hudson was now reaching 93 m.p.h. As an outfielder/DH, after hitting a whopping .385 with 9 home runs, Hudson earned first-team All-America for Division II of junior college baseball.

After his outstanding freshman season, a plethora of Division I schools had started to call. The summer after his freshman season, Hudson, yearning to improve his game, headed to Hornell, New York, to play in the Northwest Collegiate League, a league mostly for junior college players. In forty-two innings, Hudson posted a splendid 1.89 ERA.

With his confidence growing at a rapid pace, Hudson continued to excel at CVCC. As a sophomore, he was named the state's most valuable junior college player for the second season in a row. On the bump, he led the nation with 117 strikeouts and posted an 8–3 record with a 1.96 ERA. At the plate, Hudson smacked 9 home runs with 41 RBI, and 15 steals.

At this point, the longshot righty was now in contact with notable Division I schools. Alabama, Florida State, Mississippi State, and Auburn had all called and were eager to sign the junior college standout. Hudson, who grew up about twenty-five miles away from Auburn's campus, fell in love with the school and coaches after his first visit. In an interview in a 1997 issue of *Inside the Auburn Tigers*, Hudson said, "I signed as soon as Auburn offered me a scholarship."

While he wasn't promised anything, Hudson was told he would be given a chance to pitch and play outfield for the Tigers, which was all he needed to hear. From junior college to the

Southeastern Conference (SEC), Hudson, again had to prove to not only himself but to all the doubters that he could excel at baseball, no matter the competition. Hudson told me, "It was almost like I was starting all over again. New chapter, new level. I need to prove to myself and these coaches at Auburn and in the SEC that I belong here."

In his first season at Auburn, Tim came flying out of the gates. In the opening series against Virginia Commonwealth, he hit 3 home runs, including two on his parents' twenty-seventh wedding anniversary. However, shortly after the hot start, Hudson began to struggle both on the mound and at the plate. He went on to bat just twenty-two more times that season, as Auburn's coach, Hal Baird, wanted Tim to focus solely on pitching. This proved to be the right move for Hudson and the Tigers.

Behind the trust from his coaches and teammates, Tim had developed into Auburn's best pitcher by the end of the year. He led the Tigers with a 3.25 ERA and won five games, including victories over national champion LSU, Arkansas, and Ole Miss.

Heading into the offseason, Hudson was told he would be given another chance to regularly hit when he wasn't on the mound. When we spoke, he told me how he spent his free time before the next season: "I just spent a lot of hours in the cages. Me and some other guys that didn't go play summer ball—we just spent hours in there hitting. Working on hitting breaking balls, letting the ball get deep and hitting the ball to right field. Just doing the things that you need to do to be successful at the SEC level."

In the months leading up to his senior season, Hudson was anointed as the Friday night starter for the Tigers, which meant he was now the ace of the staff. In an interview with *Inside the*

Auburn Tigers, Hudson said, "Personally, I would like to get 15 wins, figuring I'm going to get about 20 starts and hit .300. That's a realistic goal for me at the plate. Hopefully, I'll hit seven or eight homers and drive in some runs. Getting to play outfield and pitch means I've already reached one of my goals for the season."

Despite setting rather lofty goals, Tim Hudson went on to have one of the best collegiate seasons in SEC history in 1997. As a DH/OF, Hudson hit .396, 18 home runs, and drove in 95 runs, breaking Frank Thomas's single-season school RBI record (Hudson's record has since been surpassed, and he currently ranks second in Auburn history for most RBI during a single-season). On the mound, he led the Tigers in all major pitching categories, finishing 15–2 with a 2.97 ERA, and 165 strikeouts. His outlandish performance earned him First-Team All-SEC, SEC Player of the Year, First-Team All-American, and the beneficiary of the renowned Rotary Smith Award, which identifies the best collegiate baseball player in America.

Not only was he the first SEC player to win the prestigious award, Hudson also became the first player to earn All-American honors at two positions: centerfield and pitcher. In a 2010 interview with the *Ledger-Enquirer*, Hal Baird, Hudson's coach at Auburn, said the following in regards to Hudson's time at Auburn: "He had a tremendous work ethic and was a fierce competitor and as confident as anyone I coached, far and away the best. He had all the intangibles."

Following his phenomenal season at Auburn, Hudson was selected by the Oakland Athletics in the sixth round of the 1997 MLB June Amateur Draft. From a statistical standpoint, Hudson should have been a surefire first-round pick, but MLB scouts looked at him as just a great college player and nothing beyond that. This, of course, was just fuel to Hudson's fire.

In 1996, the year prior to Hudson's draft, the Oakland Athletics won just 78 games, and finished third in the AL West. Part of the reason for the team's lack of success was their pitching. Out of fourteen AL teams, Oakland finished thirteenth in hits allowed and strikeouts. With that said, pitching was a main priority for the organization. Despite being selected within the first six rounds of the draft, Hudson was actually the eighth pitcher drafted by the Athletics. Even with the team picking a handful of pitchers before him, Hudson kept the same mindset he's had since his youth. In our conversation, he said, "I'm going to prove to the organization that I'm better than all of them. Even though I was a lot smaller, probably wasn't the strongest, and didn't throw as hard as the guys they drafted ahead of me."

Oakland was desperate for good pitching, so management informed their new talent that each of them would have the chance to move up quickly through the farm system if they show flashes of major league talent. "That was all I needed to hear. I was going to get a fair chance to establish myself and move up through the organization."

Hudson took this incredible opportunity and ran with it. In 1997, playing in the rookie Northwest League as a member of the Southern Oregon Timberjacks, Hudson appeared in eight games and posted a record of 3–1 with a 2.51 ERA. He had 37 strikeouts in just 28.2 innings of work, which led the A's to move up to high-A ball the following season.

Now with the Modesto A's, Hudson was nearly flawless. Again appearing in eight games, five of them as the starting pitcher, the righty went 4–0 with a 1.67 ERA. In four of those appearances, spanning from April 19 to May 3, Hudson pitched 12 straight no-hit, no-run innings. Not only did his success lead to another promotion, but coaches had started to take notice. In a 1998 interview with the *Contra Coast Times*, Huntsville Stars (Oakland's AA team) pitching coach Bert Bradley, when asked about Hudson, said, "If I hadn't seen him in spring training, I would have expected a guy about six foot three, weighing 215 pounds." Bradley went on to say, "He looks like a second basemen or something like that, but when you see him pitch, you change your whole mindset. His makeup is outstanding. You couldn't draw it up any better. He has tenacity. He's a bulldog, and he loves to pitch."

By 1999, barely standing six feet high and weighing 160 pounds, Hudson was with the Vancouver Canadians, Oakland's AAA team. Just one call away from the big leagues. In his eight starts with the Canadians, Hudson, again, could not be stopped. He went 4–0 and struck out sixty-one batters in his forty-nine innings of work.

Over in Oakland, things weren't going so great for the Athletics pitching staff. By June, the starting pitchers were 17–20 with an abysmal 5.03 ERA. Oakland General Manager Billy Beane was ready to switch things up. On June 8, 1999, Tim Hudson was promoted to the majors and was set to make his MLB debut against the San Diego Padres. He said, "Now I'm with the big boys, and I need to show everybody that I belong here."

In his opening start, Hudson put on a show in front of the San Diego crowd. In five innings of work, the Auburn standout struck out eleven batters, which is still an Oakland Athletics record for most strikeouts in a major league debut. After a few more dazzling performances, the new Oakland star was up against the biggest test of his young baseball career. On a July afternoon in Arizona, the undersized, 160-pound kid from Alabama was squaring off against Randy Johnson, the six foot ten, 225-pound stud, who had already established himself as arguably the best pitcher in the game. Up to this point in his career, Johnson had been selected for five All-Star games and was the recipient of the 1995 AL Cy Young Award. Johnson would later go on to finish his career with ten All-Star appearances and five total Cy Young Awards, including one that season in 1999. Instead of being nervous, Hudson looked at this chance as a his own "coming out party." He said, "If I can come out here and hold my own against Randy Johnson, it will just legitimize me being here in the big leagues."

"Big Unit Is Downsized as A's Hudson Prevails" headlined the *Contra Coast Times* on the day after the game. The twenty-three-year-old rookie defeated the strikeout king Johnson in a legendary performance. Hudson pitched all the way into the ninth inning, giving up 3 hits and 0 runs. After Oakland's 2–0 victory, Athletics manager Art Howe expressed his confidence in his new pitcher. "He's the one guy on our staff who I thought could match Randy for zeroes," Howe said of Hudson. "And he not only did that but went one better."

Howe later went on to say, "When a pitcher faces Johnson, he knows he is going to have to be on top of his game. [Hudson] got ahead and used all his pitches. He put on a clinic. He dealt with everything, knowing he had no margin for error." A one-time longshot who was disregarded by all collegiate programs, Tim Hudson had arrived.

In August, Oakland traveled across the country to face off against one of the best teams in the league, the Boston Red Sox, in a crucial four-game series. Both teams were in the playoff hunt, so every inning, every at-bat, and every pitch was pivotal.

After Boston won two of the first three contests, Oakland turned to their rookie, who would be facing off against Pedro Martinez. "Pedro was a guy I idolized," Hudson told me, but as someone who loves to compete, he made sure to stay focused. "As a competitor, you enjoy having head-to-head matchups against the best around."

If you are an avid fan of baseball, you probably are aware of Pedro's 1999 season. The National Baseball Hall of Famer finished the year at 23–4 with a 2.07 ERA and 313 strikeouts. He led the AL in all three categories, giving him the pitching triple crown, and, of course, the 1999 AL Cy Young Award. However, one of those four losses came on an August night against Hudson. That's right—with Dominican flags flying all over Fenway Park and fans going wild, Oakland defeated the Sox, 6–2. Although Martinez struck out eleven batters in seven innings, Hudson came out on top, throwing eight innings with 7 strikeouts and just 1 earned run. Following the game, in an interview with *The Boston Globe*, Oakland A's second basemen Randy Velarde said about Hudson, "This kid doesn't flinch. I'm sure everybody was thinking Pedro, Pedro, Pedro. And he ignored that and threw well. It seems like he has a flair for the big game." Within his first fourteen career starts, Hudson had defeated two of the best pitchers to ever walk this Earth.

Oakland's blooming star finishing his rookie campaign at 11–2 with a 3.23 ERA. The following season, Hudson made his first All-Star game, and wound up winning a league-high 20 games. He finished runner-up in the AL Cy Young Award voting to, you guessed it, Pedro Martinez.

From 2000–04, Hudson had established himself as the ace of the Athletics, and a premier pitcher in the game. During that span, he won 81 games and finished in the top-ten for the AL

Cy Young Award voting on three separate occasions. I asked Tim how he prepared for his battles. He said he used a lot of visualization techniques to plan out his next start. He would come up with a game plan against each hitter, zoning in on their strengths and weaknesses.

"I would visualize, in my head, me making great pitches. Visualizing the ball flight, visualizing the action on the pitches being exactly what I want," he said. "If you think about the right things over and over again, it seems a lot easier to go out there and execute them." Again, we saw this in Mike Modano's story. Visualization and mindfulness are the most eminent performance-enhancers that are often overlooked. Not only does this method work for an athlete, but anyone who strives for success. The more you think about positive outcomes, the more likely they are to come true.

Hudson also noted that having a good relationship with failure is vital for anyone who aspires to be great in any particular field. After a bad game, Hudson would go back, check the film, and reevaluate his game plan so that the next time he comes across a similar situation, he could adjust as necessary. "You have to be able to learn from your failures, learn from your mistakes, but not get overwhelmed to the point where it is dragging you down."

In December of 2004, Hudson started a new chapter in his MLB career when he was traded to the Atlanta Braves. As a member of the Braves, Hudson continued to dominate opposing hitters. On August 6, 2005, he won his one hundredth career game in an 8–1 victory over the St. Louis Cardinals. The following January, he was named to the Team USA roster for the 2006 World Baseball Classic.

In 2008, after getting off to another fantastic start, Hudson was faced with the biggest challenge of his career. In a July 23 start against the Florida Marlins at Dolphins Stadium, Hudson was taken out of the game after six scoreless innings and just 68 pitches. He assumed that it was just a forearm strain that stemmed from throwing an abundance of split-finger fastballs in that particular outing. As time went on, the discomfort continued, and Hudson was forced to make a decision: continue with the pain and hope it wears off or have surgery.

On August 2, 2008, Hudson informed everyone that he would be undergoing Tommy John ligament transplant surgery on his pitching elbow. He would miss the remainder of the 2008 season and a good chunk of the 2009 year as well. A major procedure that takes nine months to a year to fully recover from, Tommy John surgery could be detrimental to his pitching career. While the surgery is often a success with major league pitchers, some players' careers have been flipped upside down after going under. Hudson, then thirty-three, was in danger of his best pitching days being behind him.

It should come as no surprise that Hudson stayed confident as can be. To him, this major surgery was simply a bump in the road. He said, "I'm not gonna let this be the deciding moment for when my career starts declining."

After an extensive rehab process, Hudson was back, eager to show himself and his team that he could still perform at a high level. "I'm not going to allow myself to fail," he said. "I'm going to go out there and do whatever I need to do to be successful, both physically and mentally."

On September 1, 2009, Hudson returned to the big-league mound in fashion, striking out five in a win over the Florida Marlins. He would go on to pitch in six more games, finishing the season with a 3.61 ERA. Atlanta liked what they saw in the veteran right-hander and decided to sign Hudson to a three-year extension worth twenty-eight million dollars. This proved to be a wise move for the Braves organization.

In 2010, at age thirty-four and fresh off Tommy John surgery, Tim Hudson had plausibly his best season in the majors. He was named to his third All-Star team and finished the season with a record of 17–9 and a 2.83 ERA, his lowest since 2003. He finished fourth in Cy Young voting and was named 2010 NL Comeback Player of the Year.

Hudson won sixteen games in each of his next two seasons, and, in 2014, now a member of the San Francisco Giants, made his fourth All-Star team. He capped off that season by helping the Giants defeat the Kansas City Royals in the 2014 World Series. Tim would go on to play one more season for San Francisco before finally hanging up the cleats.

Remember those seven pitchers that Oakland drafted ahead of Hudson? They combined to win just thirteen games over the entirety of their MLB careers. In fact, among the near eight hundred pitchers selected that June, no one had a higher WAR (wins above replacement, a stat used to sum up "a player's total contributions to his team") than Hudson. During Hudson's sixteen years in the MLB, nobody in the sport won more games than the undersized, skinny, right-hander who received no offers from any Division I programs after graduating high school.

From 1999–2015, the years in which Tim Hudson played in the MLB, nobody won more games than the undersized right-handed pitcher from Alabama (222).

Nowadays, Hudson continues to spread positivity. In 2009, he and his family established the "Hudson Family Foundation," which positively impacts hundreds of children and adults in Alabama. About three years ago, Tim and his wife started the Legends Club, which, according to the foundation's website, "focuses on building self-esteem, pride, and hope in school-age children who are battling to overcome challenges in their lives." The club acknowledges local elementary school students for being great students, friends to their peers, and sons and daughters. The recipients receive a certificate and a Legends Award Champion's Box, which includes Thanksgiving dinner for them and their family.

Spreading positivity does more than help others. According to Lisa R. Yanek, MPH, and colleagues of Johns Hopkins Medicine, "People with a family history of heart disease who also had a positive outlook were one-third less likely to have a heart attack or other cardiovascular event within five to twenty-five years than those with a more negative outlook."

According to findings from a 2016 Harvard T.H. Chan School of Public Health study published in *The Harvard Gazette*, "Women who were optimistic had a significantly reduced risk of dying from several major causes of death—including cancer, heart disease, stroke, respiratory disease, and infection—over an eight-year period compared with women who were less optimistic."

We also know from a University of Kansas study that the simple act of smiling, even if it is fake, can actually reduce heart rate and blood pressure in times of stress.

However, it's not enough to think positive. We also need to be extremely cautious of the information that we absorb from external sources. The news we see on TV is often gloom-ridden, cynical, and bleak. Graham Davey, a professor emeritus of psychology at Sussex University in the UK, supervised a study on how negative news can engineer a change in our emotions. Davey compiled three groups who were each shown fourteen minutes of news on the television. One group witnessed positive, uplifting stories, another observed neutral-material, and the third group watched negative, pessimistic, information. After the experiment, Davey and his team concluded the third group experienced more anxiety and sadness and showed signs of dramatizing personal worry.

So smile more, take time out of your day to project positive outcomes, spread your knowledge to those around you, and be vigilant of the stories that you engage with. If you do those four things on a consistent basis, you will be light-years ahead of the bulk of society.

I would like to wrap up Tim's chapter with a Mark Twain quote: "It's not the size of the dog in the fight, it's the size of the fight in the dog."

Paramount Points

- No matter what the circumstance, *think positive.*

- Project positive outcomes for your future.

- Avoid captivating negative content.

- Seek out the silver lining in every situation.

- Approaching each day with an optimistic mindset has proven to positively impact our health.

CHAPTER ELEVEN

Be You

Growing up in Dayton, Oregon, about twenty-five miles southwest of Portland, Paige VanZant's adoration of recreational activities started at a very young age. As a blossoming adolescent, her hobbies included fishing, hunting, and riding dirt bikes to name a few. Her parents, Steve and Rachel, owned a dance studio, where Paige would often practice dancing ballet, jazz, and hip hop. "There are certain lessons that you don't quite learn from your parents teaching you," VanZant said. "Joining something like ballet, it taught me discipline, determination, drive. I definitely attribute a lot of my success to dance, especially my maturity at a young age. It helped me put values to what I was doing early on."

Whether it was catching the biggest fish or being the most polished on the dance floor, VanZant always strived to be the best. "I didn't wanna be the best girl on the team," she said. "I wanted to be the best in the room."

Despite her eagerness to excel in a multitude of fields as a child, VanZant was forced to face a major obstacle during her freshman year of high school. At a modest five feet tall, VanZant was one of the shortest students in the school and a victim of bullying. Her mother, Rachel, would often stop by the school to make sure her daughter was in good spirits. Rachel, in an interview with the *Reno Gazette-Journal* in 2014, said, "I just told her to be strong and positive and eventually it would pass, and she'd get through it. I think people just saw that she had a good spirit and kept her head up high and was happy and for whatever reason there were a few girls who that bothered. It was their goal in life to bring her down."

After a rough first year of high school, VanZant and her family relocated to Sparks, Nevada, where she enrolled at TMCC High School. As they settled in, VanZant was on the hunt to find a new dance studio to mold her skills. However, she stumbled across a gym owned by Ken Shamrock, a UFC Hall of Fame member, widely touted as not only one of the best to do it but a pioneer in the sport. It was here VanZant found her passion. She started out training in boxing and later took on other forms of martial arts. In our conversation, VanZant said her dance career played a vital role in her development as a fighter. "Because of dance, I knew how to work hard," she told me. "I knew what it took to be successful."

Although she makes it look easy today, VanZant wasn't what we would call a "natural" with the gloves. In fact, she actually lost her first three boxing matches. "I knew that you don't win everything," VanZant said. "I went against girls who had way more experience than me. They were better, but you don't let those things losses defines you. You just keep working hard and know you're inching closer and closer to success."

Having chatted with numerous athletes, it's obvious that having a positive mindset is crucial when striving for success in all walks of life. However, what stood out to me about VanZant was her emphasis on avoiding comparison and the importance on focusing on being the best version of yourself.

When I asked the UFC star if she had a role model in the fight game when she first started out, VanZant spoke on the negativity you bring yourself when you aspire to be someone else. "I wanna be the best me that I can be," she said. "I'm not going to try and emulate anyone else's style because that's an insult to my body and the work that I've put into it."

What started out simply as an activity to pass the time, VanZant's fighting abilities quickly caught the eyes of her coaches at Shamrock's gym, The Lion's Den. After a few years of training, VanZant's instructors had a proposition for the teenager. "When I turned eighteen, they asked if I would take a fight, and I said, 'Yeah,' " she told the *New York Post* in 2014. "I won it, and all of the sudden there was all this interest and all these opportunities. I had just one amateur fight, then my coach got a call for a pro fight for me. I thought about it and said, 'If I'd fight anyway, I might as well get paid for it.' " It should be noted that her first amateur fight lasted just 50 seconds. VanZant forced her opponent, Morgan Hunter, to submit when she put her in a rear-naked chokehold.

Two months following her amateur debut, VanZant turned professional. After three fights, VanZant was 2–1. She had already broken an opponent's arm and was even training against men at Wanderlei Silva's gym in Las Vegas. On April 6, 2013, VanZant stepped into the octagon and beat Courtney Himes in the first round at Brownson Arena in Colorado. The feisty VanZant had Himes in a headlock that left the Grand Junction fighter temporarily unconscious.

That December, following a training session, VanZant received a text message that would change her life. The message read, "Hey Paige, can you call me?" The curious VanZant phoned the unknown number and listened carefully as a male voice said, "Can you go somewhere where nobody can hear us?" Confused, VanZant asked who was on the other line.

The mysterious voice turned out to be the president of the UFC, Dana White. White had heard about VanZant's immediate success in the fight game and asked if she was interested in being a part of *The Ultimate Fighter*, a reality television show that helped put the UFC on the map by finding the next big fighters. VanZant had her contract acquired by the UFC. She would now compete against fifteen other strawweight fighters for a shot at a UFC Championship. "Making it to UFC was my biggest dream and biggest goal," VanZant told the *New York Post*. "I knew I would make it happen. I thought I'd need to put two or three more wins under my belt before that would be a possibility, but when I got that phone call it was one of the best moments of my life. I knew I deserved it, and I know I'm going to wow a lot of people."

Since that Dana White phone call, VanZant sure has wowed a lot of spectators. After being announced as a cast member of *The Ultimate Fighter*, the Sparks native was ruled ineligible for the show because alcohol was allowed in the Ultimate Fighter house, and VanZant couldn't legally drink yet.

This led to her UFC debut being delayed until November 22, 2014. In "UFC's Fight Night: Edgar vs Swanson," VanZant defeated Kailin Curran in the third round with a TKO (technical knockout). After the victory, VanZant acknowledged how being unable to compete on *The Ultimate Fighter* was actually a blessing in disguise. "It was perfect," she told the *Reno Gazette-Journal*. "I had eighteen months of downtime without the show. It allowed me to focus on getting better and focus on my skills."

Her epic performance led to "Fight of the Night" honors, giving VanZant a $50,000 bonus. This was just the second time in UFC history that the "Fight of the Night" award went to a female.

On August 27, 2016, at "UFC on Fox: Maia vs. Condit," VanZant knocked out Bec Rawlings in the second round with a perfectly landed flying head kick and a storm of punches. She was credited with her first-ever Performance of the Night award.

In her most recent bout, VanZant defeated Rachael Ostovich via submission at "UFC Fight Night: Cejudo vs. Dillashaw," in

January 2019. Following the victory, VanZant announced she had suffered an arm injury while training for UFC 236. She was forced to withdraw from the event and prepared to undergo her third surgery on her right arm. VanZant originally broke her arm in a match against Jessica-Rose Clark at "UFC Fight Night: Stephens vs. Choiin," in January 2018. That hitch in her career required two surgeries, and now she faces another procedure. When I asked Paige about injuries, the twenty-five-year-old flyweight said, "It's okay to be mad, disappointed, and frustrated. If you weren't frustrated or angry, then you don't want it bad enough. I know that I'll keep moving forward and do whatever it takes to heal myself and get back to fighting."

VanZant's TKO of Kailin Curran earned her "Fight of the Night" honors, making her the second woman in UFC history to win the award. The other was Ronda Rousey in UFC 168.

Aside from knocking opponents out in the octagon, VanZant has also developed a career in the modeling industry. She has modeled for Nike and Columbia Sportswear. Possibly her biggest accomplishment in the modeling world came in 2019 when she was selected as one of the models to appear in the 2019 Sports Illustrated Swimsuit Issue. The SI Swimsuit Edition has been published every year since 1964 and is considered the holy grail of magazines for fashion models, celebrities, and athletes.

As a fighter, model, and author (check out her biography, *Rise: Surviving the Fight of My Life*), VanZant has rapidly emerged as one of the most well-known female athletes in America. Her Instagram account, @paigevanzant, has amassed over two million followers. Social media plays a pivotal role in the lives of teenagers, and I was curious to get Paige's thoughts on the negative effects it can have on youth. According to *The Washington Post*, a report from the National Center for Education Statistics said that "20 percent of students between the ages of twelve and eighteen were bullied during the 2016–17 school year." The article went on the state that "among those students who faced bullying, 15 percent said they were bullied online or by text, a 3.5 percentage point jump from the 2014–15 school year." It was also reported that girls faced online bullying nearly three times more than boys.

This is the direct result of teenage girls criticizing their peers' appearance, lifestyle, and even the amount of likes they get on one of their photos. Lauren Paul, founder of the Kind Campaign, an internationally recognized nonprofit organization that brings awareness and healing to the negative and lasting effects of girl-against-girl bullying, opened up about her experience with teenage girls. In a 2019 PBS article, Paul recalled "meeting one girl who was obsessive about her social media accounts because a group of girls excluded her if she did not get enough likes or follows in any given week. She went so far as to painstakingly create fake profiles just to meet her quota."

VanZant, who is nationally recognized for her physical appearance, said regarding her own social media account, "I think it's important for people to realize that social media is a false reality. I want people to know that when you look at my Instagram, it's 100 percent a false reality of who I am, what I'm doing, and what I look like." VanZant went on to state that, "Everybody is just putting their best self forward, and nobody is their best self 100 percent of the time. You don't post yourself breaking down or having a bad day. So when you look at my social media and see these great, amazing pictures, that's only me 1 percent of the time. The rest of the 99 percent of my day is me sweating, training hard, and [at times] breaking down."

VanZant concluded this section in our conversation by highlighting the importance of that 99 percent, stating that the hardworking, sweaty, emotional VanZant is "the thing that my family loves me for and my husband loves me for." And VanZant wants all who have been bullied to know that "the only reason someone puts you down is because you have something that they want."

"So how can we instill confidence in these young girls who struggle with external sources bringing them down?," I asked her. While she admitted to even struggling at times with her own confidence, VanZant insisted on the value of avoiding comparison. Just like she circumvents from molding her fighting style around another individual, VanZant does her best to carry this approach into all aspects of her life. "Don't ever compare your Chapter One to someone else's Chapter Twenty," she said. VanZant has been fighting for over ten years now, so her workouts are more polished then someone who is just starting out. We all have to start somewhere, and, although we may not enjoy the struggle of new challenges, it does no good to compare your journey to someone else's.

VanZant and I ended on our chat by speaking on life as a whole. In sports and other arenas, you can't always win. Rather than beating herself down, VanZant looks at losses as stepping-stones for what is to come. "Knowing that when I lose, it's a part of my purpose," she said. "It's a part of me growing, it's a part of sharing my story, but it's not who I am."

Her final words of wisdom revolved around being comfortable in the uncomfortable. Whether you are fighting in a cage against another human being or simply walking down the street, "You're never going to be able to fully control what's going on, and you have to be okay with that."

Søren Kierkegaard, a Danish philosopher who lived during the nineteenth century, was ahead of his time in terms of recognizing the psychology behind bullying, trolling, and all forms of hate. Kierkegaard, who also advocated for keeping a journal to jot down your thoughts, said, "There is a form of envy of which I frequently have seen examples, in which an individual tries to obtain something by bullying. If, for instance, I enter a place where many are gathered, it often happens that one or another right away takes up arms against me by beginning to laugh; presumably he feels that he is being a tool of public opinion. But lo and behold, if I then make a casual remark to him, that same person becomes infinitely pliable and obliging. Essentially it shows that he regards me as something great, maybe even greater than I am: but if he can't be admitted as a participant in my greatness, at least he will laugh at me. But as soon as he becomes a participant, as it were, he brags about my greatness."

An individual only tries to intimidate or pester another human when they long for the thing in that person they ridicule. From personal experience, you can tell how well-off an individual is in life by the amount of time it takes that person to criticize another soul. Those who are truly happy and confident in their own skin do not waste one second of their existence denouncing someone else. So, next time you find yourself either observing a form of bullying or being a victim to hatred, just remember that the person committing the distasteful act is the one who is unhappy with themselves. Never let a hater dictate how you see yourself!

As far as comparing one's self to others goes, most will struggle with at one point or another. But why do we do it?

Social psychologist Leon Festinger tried to explain this concept in the 1950s when he published his social comparison theory in the *Journal of Human Relations*. In his work, Festinger said, "There exists, in the human organism, a drive to evaluate his opinions and abilities," followed by, "To the extent that objective and non-social means are not available, people evaluate their opinions and abilities by comparing respectively with opinions and abilities of others." So he asserts it's totally normal for humans to compare themselves to others. Festinger then breaks social comparison into two categories: upward comparison and downward comparison. Upward comparison is when we compare ourselves to people we think are better than us, and downward comparison is when we liken ourselves to those we view are worse off than us. While it could be argued that comparing yourself to someone "better" than you can ultimately motivate you to improve, either form of comparison will disrupt your self-evaluation and create a false understanding of what you are made to do. Looking down on someone to make you feel better will not help you move forward, and neither will craving to be like someone else.

To force you to refrain from comparison, researchers from Yonsei University, a private research university in South Korea, studied how Facebook users' perceptions of others shaped their emotions, social comparison orientation, and psychological well-being. When the group viewed another's life who was deemed as "successful" or "well-off," there were two primary reactions. A handful of participants had a stronger ability-based social comparison orientation, while others possessed a powerful opinion-based social comparison orientation. Those who fell under the ability-based social comparison orientation showed a decrease in physical well-being due to a boost in contrastive emotions like depression and envy. According to the Yonsei University website, if the social media users had "a stronger opinion-based social comparison orientation, their psychological well-being increases via increased feelings of upward assimilative emotions (e.g., optimism and inspiration) or decreased feelings of upward contrastive emotions (e.g., depression and envy) toward the comparison other."

According to scientist and relationship expert Clarissa Silva, social media has not only been associated with a decrease in social skills, but it has also proven to increase feelings of loneliness, envy, anxiety, depression, and narcissism. Silva conducted a study, interviewing highly active adult social media users. She found that 60 percent of these individuals admitted that social media has made a mark on their self-esteem in a negative way.

How we perceive our personal journey and information we absorb is everything. It is the difference between feeling optimistic or depressed. The same situation that has us feeling joyful can also have us feeling despair, and it is solely based off how we view it.

Paramount Points

- Avoid any sort of comparison.

- Comparing yourself to another individual is a major disservice to yourself and all the work you have put in.

- Comparisons lead to negative thoughts and emotions.

- There is only one you, and that's awesome.

- Social media provides us with an unrealistic portrayal of a user's actual life.

- You never know what someone is going through, so be pleasant. Kindness always prevails.

- Never let a hater own space in your head. Haters hate because they are insecure and jealous.

CHAPTER TWELVE

Identify Your "Why"

In 1975, Jimmie Kenneth Johnson was born in El Cajon, California. By age five, Johnson was racing 50cc motorcycles. "Being a professional racer was definitely in my head at a super young age," Johnson told me. "There was an experience on that dirt bike when I started riding at five. That's where the passions come from."

Jimmie's father, Gary, told the *Tampa Bay Times* in 2002 that Jimmie started racing "Because it was cute. Every kid got a trophy and it was just fun." However, as Jimmie grew older, his love for speeding around a track and competing against others continued to elevate. "It kept growing and growing," Gary Johnson said. "By the time he was eight, he had a factory ride and we were traveling the country racing motorcycles."

Jimmie, whose father drove trucks and operated heavy machinery for a living while his mother, Cathy, worked as a school bus driver, was a gifted racer from the jump. Every summer, the Johnson family spent a good chunk of time in the family van driving around from race to race to watch Jimmie test his skills against other competitors around the nation. "Going fast. Racing. Competing. There's just something there that makes me feel so alive," Johnson said in our conversation. "That's what I've chased." The pursuit of a particular feeling he experienced as a child pushed Johnson to take his racing career to another level.

From 1992–97, competing in the Mickey Thompson Stadium, SCORE Desert and SODA Winter series, Johnson won six championships racing off-road trucks.

In 1996 and 1997, Johnson raced with Herzog Motorsports in the SODA series. One day, while racing in a lower division event with his squad, Johnson caught the attention of the owner of Hendrick Motorsports, Rick Hendrick. Hendrick was watching his teams compete in the premier division. Luckily for Johnson, the young racer had a day for the ages. "I had a career night," he exclaimed. "I won my races, qualified first, and did all these great things. Little did I know, he [Rick Hendrick] was sitting in the stands watching."

Hendrick, who was fascinated by how Johnson raked in many top-ten finishes despite competing in nothing close to a top-ten car, encouraged Jimmie to try out stock car racing. Jeff Gordon, a former professional stock car racer who drove for Hendricks Motorsports, was one of the first people to convince Jimmie to make the career switch. He told the *Tampa Bay Times*, "I don't know if Rick [Hendrick] and I picked him or if he picked us. It appeared to me that if you put this guy in a top-notch team and car in the Winston Cup circuit, he would get a lot out of it." Boy, did he ever.

Driven by pure adoration for the sport, Johnson flourished in his first year in the American Speed Association (ASA) circuit. In September 1998, Johnson was named the Pat Schauer Memorial Rookie of the Year, an award for the top rookie in the ASA. In the same year, he started out as a part-time driver in the NASCAR Busch Series (now Xfinity Series).

When I asked Jimmie about his original goals, the NASCAR legend said, "I felt if I could win a race, I could keep a job for a few years. That's as big as my dreams could take me. What has happened since has obviously been far more."

In 1999, Johnson won two races and finished third in the points standings. The next year, Johnson was announced as the driver for Herzog Motorsports in the Busch Series. In June 2000, Johnson, while racing in the NASCAR Busch Grand National Series' Lysol 200 at Watkins Glen International, was in a devastating crash. On lap 46, the throttle on his No. 92

ALLTEL Chevy seemed to stick open, which caused him to bounce over the turn 1 gravel trap at an outlandish speed (150 m.p.h.). His car went airborne and crashed into the Styrofoam-covered barrier. Somehow, Johnson managed to come out of the crash unmarked.

Racing around an oval-shaped, asphalt track in a stock car whose engine allows the vehicle to exceed 200 m.p.h. while also making turns that range from 36 degrees at Talladega Superspeedway to 12 degrees at Martinsville Speedway. Who in their right state of mind would put themselves in this position?

"I've always just wanted to race. I love flying around in these racecars," Johnson said. "It's just so fun."

When I brought up the fear involved in stock car racing, Johnson was quick to inform me that he doesn't try to deny fear exists. "Fear has always been a big part of my life. I don't think you ever become completely fearless," he explained. "I'm very much aware of fear and I don't live a fearless lifestyle. I think I make better decisions the more aware I am of the risks I'm taking."

By being aware of his fears, Johnson is able to confront them head-on and accept them for what they are. Fear is not natural, as it is solely created in our mind. So, by understanding the consequences and great potential for injury, Johnson looks at his fears in a different light. Rather than focusing on the bad, which would lead to a cycle of negative thoughts, Johnson's acceptance of the dangers in his profession allow for his mind to remain relaxed and focused.

In 2002, Johnson began racing full-time in the Winston Cup Series. In April, while lounging in their living room in Concord, NC, Jimmie Johnson's parents glued their eyes to the TV and watched their son place first in the NAPA Auto Parts 500 at Auto Club Speedway. This was Johnson's first-ever Winston Cup victory and just his thirteenth career start. Edging out Kurt Busch by approximately six car-lengths, Johnson, who was overcome with joy during his victory celebration, spun around the track and onto the grass before ultimately blowing out the engine and transmission. "Heck, yeah," he told *The Courier*, after the milestone win. "You always think you've got enough ability to win, but you never know until you get out there and do it."

In 2006, Johnson won his first Daytona 500, inarguably the most prestigious race in NASCAR. From 2006–10, Jimmie Johnson rattled off five-straight Cup Series championships, becoming the first and only driver in NASCAR history to accomplish this feat. In 2013, not only did he win his second Daytona 500, but Johnson also captured his sixth championship. Three years later, in 2016, he joined Richard Petty and Dale Earnhardt as the only three racers in NASCAR history to win seven championships. To date, Johnson has eighty-three career wins, which ties for the sixth most career wins of all time.

Jimmie Johnson is the only driver in NASCAR history to win five consecutive championships.

So besides becoming aware of his fears, how does a man achieve this much success in racing? "We call it seat time," the seven-time champion told me. "The more time you spend in the seat driving, the better you become. The vehicle becomes an extension of you." Johnson aims to spend as much time in the car as possible, but because of the high costs, the driver can't just practice laps around a course whenever he wants.

The cost of an engine for these high-powered whips can range anywhere from $45,000 to $80,000. The transition to electronic fuel injection systems adds on about $10,000 to the electric bill each week. Keep in mind the brakes and rotors are another $20,000. According to Jacksonville.com, "keeping a 200-m.p.h. racecar at full-speed costs about $50,000 a week for parts and pieces."

This is why NASCAR drivers use racing simulators to develop their skills behind the wheel. According to ESPN, "A simulator uses huge screens, with the seating mechanism in the middle of a dark room, plus an adjacent room for engineers to watch and download data." The simulators are so realistic that some drivers have actually puked after a few laps. The seat moves as if you are in the middle of a real-life race, and the team is able to toggle with the settings to create mock scenarios.

Aside from practice directly related to his profession, Johnson is a triathlete. In his free time, the NASCAR legend enjoys swimming, biking, and running. He enjoys living an active lifestyle and puts a heavy emphasis on eating right and getting enough sleep. "The mindset within being fit is the mindset of a racer," he tells me. "The worlds are parallel."

In April 2019, Johnson completed the Boston Marathon, finishing with a time of 3:09:07, which was good for 641st in the male 40–44 class.

Notice how Jimmie attributed getting the proper amount of sleep as a key to his indelible success. The American Academy of Sleep Medicine studied over four thousand young people (eleven to seventeen years old) and found that those who sleep an average of six or fewer hours per night increase their odds of suffering from major depression. Getting the appropriate measure of sleep is vital for our overall health, happiness, and brainpower. Numerous studies have demonstrated how sleep helps regulate our emotions, keep our memory solid, control our weight, and much more. If you want to operate like a well-oiled machine with high energy and a brain operating at a top-notch level, make sure you get eight hours of rest every single night.

Not only does Johnson go to extremes to make sure he is physically ready to compete at the top level, but the forty-three-year-old always makes sure to heighten his focus before a competition. "For a race in general, it's more about just being in the right mindset, which is kind of an open and peaceful mind," he said. "It's easy to carry aggression into the car, make mistakes, or overdrive the vehicle. I'm really just trying to tune in and become centered in some ways." With most races lasting three-and-a-half hours, consisting of eight to ten pit stops, it is vital to be in the right state of mind to achieve success against the thirty-nine other competitors.

Through racing, Johnson and his wife, Chandra, launched The Jimmie Johnson Foundation. The foundation's focal point is funding K–12 public education. To date, the foundation has donated nearly twelve million dollars to various organizations, most notably, Habitat for Humanity, Hendrick Marrow Program, Make-A-Wish Foundation, and Victory Junction. "These are the other layers that come with it," Johnson said. "Because I am being true to myself and being who I am."

So how exactly does one identify their "why" and, by doing so, build a career and inspire millions? Johnson admitted he was lucky to find his purpose at a very young age but believes that it's never too late to find yourself. "I think ultimately it's about listening to yourself and knowing what works for you," he said. "Self-understanding is the most important thing for me. We are all wired differently. Some people have a calling." Speaking of being wired differently, Johnson's wife, Chandra, is much more intellectual. While Jimmie prefers to go skydiving or ride his mountain bike, Chandra loves to read and takes a heavy interest in art.

After graduating from the University of Oklahoma, Chandra was unsure where her business degree would take her. By keeping an open mind and putting herself in different situations, Johnson has found herself with art. After getting involved with local museums, Chandra, in 2015, started SOCO (Southern Comfort Gallery), an art space and bookshop based in Charlotte, North Carolina. The passionate visionary went from hosting pop-up exhibitions of art from all around the country to running a booming business. "A lot has happened in three years," she told *Culture Magazine*. "There were artists who were on my wish list when we first started and I thought, 'maybe I'll get them in five or seven years.' But we're working with them now, so it has grown tremendously."

So if you're fortunate to find your calling at a young age like Jimmie, never stop chasing it. But, if it takes you a little longer, don't panic. Work hard, try new things, and always be open to entering a new environment.

When Jimmie and I spoke, he was in a racing slump. Johnson had gone over twenty races without a victory, and the media began to question his ability. However, like all the great athletes, Johnson's confidence did not falter. "I always learned more from the tough times," Johnson told me. "I wanna be in the car more now than ever." Rather than running from his struggles, Johnson is attacking them head-on.

Even in 2019, Johnson continues to chase that exhilarating feeling he felt when he first climbed on a motorcycle at age five. When asked about what it has been like to compete at the highest level for over a decade, he said, "[Racing] makes me feel like a kid again. It's the only place where I'm that giddy and passionate."

Dating back to the Prohibition era, the state of Florida has always been tied with corruption and contraband trading. When prohibition was at its peak, nightclubs in the "Sunshine State" celebrated the idea of buying and selling alcohol. Floridians enjoyed throwing back drinks imported from the Caribbean islands, despite what the laws said. The *Miami New Times* recalls the roaring twenties as a time period where "liquor flowed in on the tides" of the Miami River, leading to extreme violence between gangs and law enforcement. South Florida, in particular, because of its proximity to the Caribbean, disregarded the Eighteenth Amendment like no other part of America. In order to be one step ahead of the US Coast Guard, liquor smugglers would use World War I airplane engines in their speedboats to travel to the Bahamas and collect their product to bring back to the states. Throughout the 1920s, Coast Guard patrol did not hesitate when it came to laying down the law. In 1926, E.W. "Red" Shannon, who was allegedly coming back to Florida with 170 cases of liquor, was shot and killed by the Coast Guardsmen.

However, Florida didn't just have a smuggling issue. The majority of the state's law enforcement was also anti-prohibition and would look the other way when citizens illegally transported liquor. *The Orlando Sentinel* said, that prohibition was "as unpopular as the plague," citing that even the Orlando mayor would be seen at clubs like the Flamingo

Café, consuming liquor with members of the community. Prisoners held in the Dade County Jail were released by the Florida police at night to go back to their bootlegging business. In return, a certain percentage of these culprits' income from smuggling would go directly into the hands of the officials who let them out. According to RecoveryFirst.org, in 1927, "prohibition agents conducted mass arrests of deputies and police officers of Broward County, in an attempt to crack down on what the *Associated Press* called 'one of the biggest liquor conspiracies in the country.' "

Despite the severe actions taken by the federal government, it was truly impossible to slow down the flow of liquor in Florida. Even after Congress passed the Twenty-first Amendment to legalize the production, transportation, and sale of alcohol, the precedent in Florida had been set. Drug smugglers in the area had power over the law. If you want to learn more about the illegal behavior that took place in Florida during the twentieth century, read up on gangsters like Al Capone and Meyer Lansky.

By the 1960s, narcotics were sprinkled throughout Florida communities. However, the introduction of cocaine in the mid-80s was, by far, the most devastating time for the state. In 1986, The *Palm Beach Post* reported "The only thing that appears certain in Riviera Beach these days is the likelihood of a higher crime rate. Burglaries, drug sales, and, more recently, organized youth gangs, are all increasing police problems."

A 1987 headline in the same paper read, "Cocaine Fuels Huge Increase in Crime Rates," which was followed by some glaring statistics. The article said, "Florida's cocaine trade boosted the crime rate in 1986 as the state recorded an 11.5 percent jump in serious crimes over 1985, the third consecutive year crime has risen." According to the Florida Department of Law Enforcement, a major crime took place every 33 seconds. On average, one in twelve Floridians were victims to these deadly wrongdoings. "A murder was clocked every six-and-a-half hours, a robbery every twelve minutes, and a burglary every two minutes."

Riviera Beach in Palm Beach County actually hired nurse specialists to work with cocaine-addicted mothers and their babies. If a mother's test results came up positive for drugs or alcohol, the State Department of Health and Rehabilitative Services would be notified and immediately send in help. Early research on the effects of cocaine on newborns concluded that the babies are more likely to suffer from digestive or respiratory system problems. *The Palm Beach Post* said, "Infants exposed to drugs or alcohol are seventeen times more likely to succumb to Sudden Infant Death Syndrome."

If you go by Neighborhood Scout's Crime Index (0–100 scale, 100 being the safest of cities), Riviera Beach is at a 4. Per 1,000 residents, 13.7 Riviera Beach citizens commit violent crimes (murder, rape, assault, robbery). Members of the community have a one in seventy-three chance of being a victim in these crimes.

In 1982, Devin Devorris Hester was born in Riviera Beach. When Hester was less than six months old, his biological father was sentenced to six years in prison. According to a study published by *The Journal of the American Medical Association*, if one or both of your caregivers was incarcerated during your childhood, the odds of you suffering from anxiety, spending time in jail for a felony, not finishing high school, becoming a teen-parent, or dealing with social isolation, drastically increased. His surroundings were far from ideal, and this didn't help.

His father's jail sentence lead Hester's parents to divorce when he was still a toddler. It wasn't until Hester was in kindergarten that he was able to experience his first real memory with his dad.

Growing up in an impoverished, crime-ridden neighborhood, Hester and his brother used sports to stay off the streets. "Football was our main hobby," Hester said. "We started playing in the Boys and Girls Club, and then recreation. It was a way out."

With his mother, Juanita Brown, working around the clock to keep the lights on, Devin had to be extremely cautious the moment he stepped off the bus. "Go home, lock the door, and don't open that door for anybody," Hester recalled his mother telling him at age seven.

The Boys and Girls Club, a national organization of local chapters which provide after-school programs for young people, allowed Hester and his brother to not only develop as kids but also as athletes. "You play sports, they help you with homework, give you something to eat," he told me. "Every day, me and my brother were the last kids to leave the club." With their mother working until seven thirty, the Hester boys stayed at the Boys and Girls Club from right after school until eight in the evening every weekday.

Soon, Devin's speed while playing sports in the neighborhood caught the eyes of the other parents. It was apparent that Hester needed to start using the athletic talents he developed in the streets and at the Boys and Girls Club in a recreational league. However, it was difficult for his mother to afford putting him in a football program. Luckily for Hester, the fathers in the neighborhood helped out the family whenever they could, as they saw serious potential in him.

When he first started playing organized football, Hester's passion for the sport grew immensely. He went from being a quick kid in the neighborhood to one of the best players on the field. However, when he was ten, his mother was nearly paralyzed after suffering significant injuries in a car wreck. Two years later, Hester's father, Lenorris Sr., died of cancer. Lenorris Jr., Devin Hester's brother, told *USA Today*, "It was probably the worst pain me and him have felt."

In our conversation, Hester recollected a conversation he had with his father, just weeks before his passing. "My dad told me, 'Don't ever be like your father,' " he said. "Be better than what I did. Your father made a lot of mistakes. I've been in and out of prison. I took the wrong path. Now, I'm in a situation where I'm dying. Don't be like your father. Don't take the path I took. I want you to become somebody." From that point on, Hester's mentality changed. He had found his "why" through his father's words.

By the ninth grade, Hester's goal was clear: get to the NFL. "This is what I'm going to do," he said. "Regardless of what anybody says."

Hester started his high school football career at Palm Beach Gardens High and later transferred to Suncoast High School. On the field, Hester starred as a cornerback, wide receiver, running back, and return specialist. After a monster game during his senior year, Hester was pictured as the first "In The Spotlight" athlete in *The Palm Beach Post*. The 2001 article highlighted Hester's statistics against Oakland Park, a contest in which he rushed for 194 yards and 4 touchdowns, caught

an 82-yard touchdown pass, and even wound up throwing a
39-yard touchdown pass in the team's 48–18 victory. Below the
statistical references were a few generic questions that Hester
answered for the readers. His favorite singer at the time was
Master P. Hot, and spicy chili was listed as his favorite pig-out
food. When asked, "What will you be doing in ten years?" the
Suncoast senior wrote "Playing professional football." Finally,
under "Most Cherished Possession," was written "A picture of
his father, who died about six years ago."

Rated as the second-best cornerback in the nation by Rivals.
com, Hester received hundreds of football scholarship
offers from the top programs in the country. After careful
consideration, Hester decided to take his talents to the
University of Miami, the hottest program in the country and
winner of the National Championship in 2001.

From 2003–05, Hester excelled for the Hurricanes. In his
first season, Hester, in a game against Florida, scored with
the opening kickoff. During his sophomore season, he was
the only player in the country who recorded at least one punt
return, kickoff return, and rushing touchdown. In the 2004
Chick-Fil-A Peach Bowl, Hester returned a blocked field goal
78 yards for a touchdown, helping the 'Canes defeat Florida,
27–10. His incredible 2004 season earned him All-American
honors as kick returner by Walter Camp, the Football Writers
Association, and Sporting News.

The following season, Hester's punt return TD against Temple
gave the junior his fourth career punt return touchdown, which
ranks second all-time in the University of Miami's storied
history. Rather than staying another year, Hester decided to
declare for the NFL draft. In April 2006, Devin Hester's dream
came true. The WR/DB was selected in the second round, fifty-

seventh overall, by the Chicago Bears. Just like the fathers in his neighborhood, Hester's coaches quickly picked up on the fact that he was quick. While they didn't know exactly where Hester would primarily play, the Chicago Bears were set on making Hester a return man for their squad, a decision that end up changing the franchise's history in ways nobody anticipated.

In his NFL debut against the Green Bay Packers, Devin Hester returned a punt 84-yards for his first-ever NFL touchdown. In week six, he returned another punt for a score, helping the Bears cap off a 20-point comeback against the Arizona Cardinals, 24–23. During a road game against the New York Giants, Hester took advantage of a Jay Feely missed field goal attempt, bringing the kick back 108 yards for a touchdown, which is tied for the second-longest touchdown in NFL history. In Chicago's Week 12 contest against their NFC North division rival, Minnesota Vikings, Hester put the Bears on the board with a 45-yard punt return touchdown. The following week, Hester started the Chicago scoring party by getting his first-ever kickoff return, a 94-yard score. In that same game, with just under 8 minutes to go in regulation, Hester recorded his second career kickoff return TD, this one going for 96 yards. Just 13 weeks into his NFL career, Devin Hester set an NFL record with six touchdown returns during the regular season. His 5 punt/kickoff returns also wound up being a new record.

Hester's elite play helped the Bears finish the 2006 season with a 13–3 record, the franchise's most wins in a season since 2001. Chicago took care of business in OT against the Seattle Seahawks in the NFC Divisional Round, and, one week later, demolished the New Orleans Saints, 39–14. For the first time since 1985, the Chicago Bears were back in the Super Bowl. Chicago was set to match up against the Indianapolis Colts, who were seeking their first Super Bowl victory since 1970, when the team was known as the Baltimore Colts.

Days before the Super Bowl, the Indianapolis Colts coaching staff was bombarded with questions about how to handle Hester. Would they kick to him? How do you stop this man?

When asked about Hester and his impact on the game, Russ Purnell, special teams' coach for the Colts, admitted that the idea of facing the Florida boy has kept him up at night. "I slept about four hours for four nights [before our game]," Purnell told *The Cincinnati Enquirer* in 2007. "He's extremely talented, and his blockers are outstanding."

Indianapolis head coach Tony Dungy complimented Hester's game but specified that the Colts were ready to attack anyone. The week of the big game, Dungy told the *Orlando Sentinel*, "Devin Hester is a big concern. He's a guy that changed games. There may be a time when you kick away from him. But for the most part, we're going to kick to him. We've got to be ready to cover anyone." Maybe Purnell's lack of sleep should have alarmed Dungy a bit more...

When I asked him to recall his mindset ahead of the biggest game of his life, Hester kept it simple. While sitting at his locker, Hester would "see myself making big plays. Whether that be picking up a first down or taking a kickoff to the house. My vision was to go into the game and set the tempo. Make a big play early. My first one I get, I'm gonna do whatever it takes to get into the end zone."

On February 4, 2007, Devin Hester returned the opening kickoff in Super Bowl XLI 92 yards for a touchdown and became the first player in NFL history to return the inaugural kickoff for a score in the Super Bowl. That was the last time in the contest the Colts would directly kick to Hester. Indianapolis ultimately defeated Chicago 29–17, but Hester's performance in the big game capped off one of the best seasons ever for a return man.

The following year, Hester broke his own record, racking up 6 punt/kickoff return touchdowns in the regular season. For the second straight season, Hester was named First-Team All-Pro. In 2010, Hester made his third First-Team All-Pro while setting a new NFL record for most yards gained on punt returns on average (17.1).

Devin Hester's 19 career return touchdowns are the most in NFL history.

Hester officially walked away from the NFL in 2016. He finished his career with 19 kickoff/punt return touchdowns, which is an NFL record. 14 of those 19 returns came via punts, which is also the most in the NFL history. His 3,695 total yards gained on punts is the third highest in NFL history. "It was the passion I had. Football was all I knew," Hester told me. "That's where my heart was. I did everything around football." From growing up in one of the roughest areas in America, at one of the worst times, Devin Hester's career shows anything is possible when you have purpose for why you do what you do. Rags to riches. Tragedy to triumph.

When we identify our purpose, not only are we establishing a reason to get up every day and work hard, but we are also putting ourselves in a position to live a happier and longer life. In many Japanese cultures, the secret to experiencing a joyful, long-lasting life can be summed up in one word: Ikigai. In Japanese, *Iki*, means "to live," and *gai* is another word for "reason" and can be defined as the "reason we wake up each morning."

In a 2009 TED Talk, award-winning journalist Dan Buettner went in-depth about the idea of Ikigai. He referenced adults who have defined their Ikigai, which has led to a blissful and lengthy life. For one family man he mentions, following his passion for the outdoors and catching fish three times a week is his secret to living over one hundred years. For a 102-year-old woman, the idea of holding her great-great-granddaughter keeps her going. Teaching martial arts to his surrounding peers was a 102-year-old karate master's secret.

In 2008, researchers from Tohoku University decided to dig deeper into Ikigai. They gathered more than 50,000 adults and studied who had Ikigai in their lives as opposed to those who did not. According to MSN.com, the researchers "found that those who reported having Ikigai in their lives had reduced risks of cardiovascular diseases and lower mortality rates. Put another way, 95 percent of respondents who had Ikigai were still alive seven years after the initial survey compared to the 83 percent who didn't."

Listen to yourself. Take time out of your day to sit down and write out what makes you happy. Maybe you're chasing a particular feeling like Jimmie Johnson. Maybe it's making your parents proud or proving someone in your past wrong. Whatever it is, clearly identify it, and don't stop chasing that dream, no matter what obstacles get in your way.

Paramount Points

- Pinpoint a reason for why you do what you do.

- On days when it seems like nothing is going your way, your "why" will keep you going.

- Your "why" will increase your drive and dedication to the craft, as it gives you a cause to go after what you want.

- The only way to find out what appeals to you in this wonderful world is by going out and trying new things. Don't shy away from change or new situations. You never know what you might find out about yourself.

CHAPTER
THIRTEEN

Become Obsessed

"I got bullied," two-division champion in the UFC, Georges St-Pierre, told me. "We don't always know the cause of something, but I know that was one of the major reasons why I wanted to get into it." It, of course, means mixed martial arts.

Growing up in the minuscule municipality of Saint-Isidore in the Montérégie region of Québec, St-Pierre was often picked on at school. He was small and was constantly ridiculed by his peers for the way he walked on the balls of his feet due to his high arches.

His father, Roland St-Pierre, was a black belt in Kyokushin Karate, which is the style of martial arts that Georges started practicing at age seven. He marveled over Jean-Claude Van Damme, Steven Segal, Chuck Norris, and Arnold Schwarzenegger.

When he was ten, St-Pierre, with a few years of training under his belt, decided to put his skills to use and take on three bullies at school. "GSP," as many refer to him now, was beaten up pretty badly by the boys and ended up on the ground in disbelief. At this moment, St-Pierre knew he needed to ramp up his training habits if he ever wanted to stand a chance against the schoolboys who tormented him.

When asked about mixed martial arts (MMA), St-Pierre said, "It saved my life. I grew up with not much and had a lot of anger." This anger stemming from getting bullied and a rough home life. "I needed to put this negative energy somewhere, and I found martial arts. It gave me discipline. Martial arts teach you about discipline and respect, and that's how it helped me to become a better man."

As a teenager, St-Pierre and his buddies rented a video of the Ultimate Fighting Championship, the first MMA event held by the UFC. At this point in 1993, the UFC looked a lot different than today's sport. There were no weight classes, and the rounds had no time limits. The competitors did not wear gloves, and head-butting, which is now illegal, was very common.

The event was headlined by Royce Gracie, a Brazilian mixed martial artist. In the first round, Gracie took on Art Jimmerson, a boxer, who had over thirty professional fights to his name. Jimmerson was the bigger opponent, yet Gracie forced the seasoned fighter to concede the match. In the semi-finals, Gracie was able to get Ken Shamrock in a firm chokehold, forcing the MMA artist to submit. Gracie then defeated Gerald Gordeau in identical fashion, a rear-naked choke.

While his friends were infatuated by the violence, St-Pierre was blown away by the tactics of the UFC 1 Tournament champion.

"When I first saw Royce Gracie winning in the UFC, he really inspired me because he was smaller than everybody," St-Pierre said. "He didn't win the tournament by being stronger or bigger than his opponents. Winning the way he did really inspired me because I could see myself getting bullied at school. I saw a small guy defeating a bigger guy because of his knowledge and a technique that nobody knew at the time, which was the ground fighting [Jiu-Jitsu], and it was like a new weapon."

Drawing comparisons between himself and the professional fighter, St-Pierre passionately told his friends, "That's what I'm gonna do for a living," which led his pals to burst out in laughter. Luckily for the UFC and millions of fans around the world, the negative reaction did not affect the young teen. "I had this dream in my head of becoming World Champion. The danger in life is not setting your goals too high and never being able to reach them. It's to set your goals too low and be able to reach them." he said. "I'm not afraid to set my goals too high, because I know it will elevate me."

Once he had the dream of becoming a World Champion in the UFC, everything changed for St-Pierre. His training habits revved up. Aside from karate, St-Pierre began rehearsing wrestling, boxing, and, like Gracie, Jiu-Jitsu. "I was obsessed," GSP told me. To help me understand his obsession, St-Pierre compared his love for martial arts to poker. "When you're obsessed about something and you have a dream, it's like playing poker with other guys, except you have more chips to put in," he said. "If you're obsessed, it gives you more chips. You're willing to put more into it to obtain what you want."

Not only does an obsession for a particular field make you more prone to create goals and chase your dream, it will also force you out of your comfort zone. At age sixteen, St-Pierre would travel from Québec to New York in order to get proper Jiu-Jitsu training. "I didn't have any money," he recalled. "I risked my life to go there with [an unreliable] car that I didn't know if it was going to break in the middle of the road." St-Pierre also remembered he would often get lost in the Bronx and had trouble getting help because his English was very poor (many Québec residents speak mostly French). "I was willing to go through that," St-Pierre said. "People, sometimes, they don't want to get out of their comfort zone. You're not going to achieve what you want if you stay in your comfort zone. You need to go get it. In life, nobody will give you anything. You need to make it happen."

With the proper mindset and an obsession for the sport, St-Pierre continued to mold his skills. During his teenage years, Québec became the first province to legalize extreme fighting. Soon after, the Canadian MMA organization, Universal Combat

Challenge (UCC, eventually renamed to the TKO), was created. The UCC introduced weight classes, rounds with time limits, and made a clear "no head-butting" rule.

As a twenty-one-year-old, St-Pierre made his debut in the UCC, fighting against Ivan Menjivar in UCC 7: Bad Boyz. Known as the "Pride of El Salvador," Menjivar entered the match on a four-fight-winning streak. The fight was evenly matched through the first few minutes, but, late in the first round, GSP's vicious punches forced the referee to stop the fight. "I remember my first fight, I made $1,100," St-Pierre told me. "Which, at the time, was good!"

The top fighters in the UCC were only making $15,000 a year at most, so St-Pierre was enrolled in college courses and worked at a carpet store in addition to training around the clock. While some of the fighters had income from sponsors, St-Pierre's poor English made it difficult to attract sponsorships.

In his second career fight, St-Pierre defeated Justin Bruckmann and was crowned the UCC Welterweight Champion. Despite the immediate success, St-Pierre, juggling school, fighting, and work, struggled to make ends meet. According to a 2006 article from *The Gazette*, "He was once so broke that he had to borrow two thousand dollars from his mother while finishing his kinesiology studies at Édouard-Montpetit College in Longueuil."

"Some people, they look at me now and think I've been wealthy my whole life," St-Pierre said in our conversation. "I went the hard way, and I paid my dues."

After four wins to start his professional career, St-Pierre was given the chance of a lifetime—a scheduled fight against Pete Spratt, a UFC fighter who had most recently taken down

Robbie Lawler at UFC 42. Lawler, who entered the match undefeated in his professional career, would eventually go on to become a UFC Welterweight Champion. Spratt's confidence was sky-high, and he assumed a fight in the TKO would be a cakewalk. He was ten years older than St.-Pierre and had eighteen professional fights under his belt.

Despite the experience disadvantage, St-Pierre backs down from no man. While he performed well in each of his four previous fights, St-Pierre's showing against the rising UFC star was the best of his young career. The fight started with GSP performing a powerful double-leg takedown on Spratt, which set the tone and ultimately ended the fight. Three minutes and forty seconds into the bout, Spratt was forced to submit after St-Pierre had him in a rear-naked choke, the same move that won Royce Gracie the UFC Tournament in 1993.

After the epic performance, the UFC had officially taken notice of Georges St-Pierre. Two months later, GSP made his UFC debut, heading off to Las Vegas to compete in UFC 46. St-Pierre was up against the high ranked Karo Parisyan, who he defeated by unanimous decision. The payout for this one was six thousand dollars—three thousand for competing and three thousand for the victory.

Following his UFC debut, St-Pierre needed just 1 minute and 42 seconds to defeat his next opponent, Jay Hieron. Standing with a professional record of 7–0, the UFC decided that St-Pierre would be given the chance to fight Matt Hughes for the vacant UFC Welterweight Championship. Hughes, who St-Pierre admired while growing up, entered the fight with a 36–4 record. He had been professionally fighting since Georges was a teenager and was established as one of the best fighters in the UFC. Unfortunately for GSP, he was defeated by Hughes, who was crowned UFC Welterweight Champion after getting St-Pierre in an armbar.

Despite the loss, St-Pierre's obsession and adoration for the sport did not slow him down. When I brought up the loss in our conversation, GSP quoted the late Cus D'Amato, Mike Tyson's trainer: "Fear is like fire. You can make it work for you: it can warm you in winter, cook your food when you're hungry, give you light when you are in the dark, and produce energy. Let it go out of control and it can hurt you, even kill you... Fear is a friend of exceptional people." Georges went on to say, "My failure has always been my worst fear, but every time I lose, I learn from it." St-Pierre admitted he should not have put Hughes on a pedestal, realizing "He has two arms, two legs, and is no different than me."

Like all elite athletes, GSP bounced back with ease to win four straight fights, and he gave himself the opportunity at another shot of becoming a World Champion.

In March 2006, St-Pierre was set to go to war against B.J. Penn. Penn entered the bout winning five out of his last six fights, including a submission of Matt Hughes.

The training schedule ahead of the fight may appear excessive, but, for an obsessed, focused, and determined fighter like St-Pierre, immense success calls for taking training to extreme measures. Training was twice a day, six times a week. On Mondays, St-Pierre would focus on weight-training. Tuesdays were for private kickboxing lessons, while Wednesdays were reserved for boxing. On Thursdays and Sundays, GSP would work on wrestling. Knowing Penn is a Jiu-Jitsu phenomenon, St-Pierre would drive seven hours to New York every three weeks and train at the Gracie Jiu-Jitsu Academy.

"You need to work hard, develop the skill and knowledge, while also making the right life decisions," St. Pierre said.

Prior to the weigh-in, St-Pierre cut out all carbs and sodium. By avoiding pasta, rice, potatoes, and salt, the body is able to get rid of water at a faster rate than when one consumes a heavy amount of carbohydrates and salt.

During the night of the fight against Penn, St-Pierre's hometown was a madhouse. If you wanted a seat at Champs Sports Bar and restaurant on St. Laurent Blvd., you better have reserved a table several days in advance. At Tristar Gym where St-Pierre trains, friends of GSPs gathered around to watch the hometown hero compete in Las Vegas, where fans paid nearly five hundred dollars to witness it in person.

"It's so big there, it's too emotional," Georges's mother, Paulyne St-Pierre, informed *The Gazette* in 2006, "I prefer to watch it in the comfort of the living room."

Unlike his two previous fights, GSP's fight against Penn went the distance. Luckily for the Canadian star, St-Pierre was named the winner by split decision, improving his record to 12–1. Following the fight, Myriane, Georges's sister, was overcome with emotion, bursting into tears over her big brother's win. Not only had he defeated one of the best extreme fighters in the sport, St-Pierre had earned a rematch with Matt Hughes for the UFC Welterweight Championship. This time around, St-Pierre made sure he wouldn't make the same mistakes he made two years earlier.

On November 18, 2006, Georges St-Pierre's dream of becoming a World Champion had come to fruition. One minute and 25 seconds into the second round, GSP avenged his lone loss, winning by TKO. St-Pierre became just the second Canadian-born fighter to hoist a UFC title belt. After the victory, UFC President, Dana White, called Georges "The most dominant Welterweight Champion of all time." Matt Hughes was also quoted, saying, according to *The Edmonton Journal*, that St-Pierre "is the future of the sport, there's no doubt about that." Along with a fancy new welterweight championship belt, St-Pierre earned $80,000 for the fight. Not bad for a few minutes of work.

Following his title win over Hughes, St-Pierre would go on to win twelve of his next thirteen fights. In 2013, he retired as the defending Welterweight Champion. St-Pierre broke the record for most victories in title bouts, while defending his title nine straight times. When I asked him about all of his success, the UFC legend kept it simple: "Satisfaction for an athlete is the end. I stayed hungry and obsessed."

That hunger and obsession never wavered, even when St-Pierre was retired. While he traveled the world and studied paleontology, a field that he had been passionate about ever since he was a kid, Georges continued to practice martial arts, training once or twice a day.

Four years after announcing his retirement, St-Pierre declared he would be returning to the sport. This time, he was slated to fight Michael Bisbing for the UFC Middleweight Championship. Up to this point, only three fighters in the history of the sport, Randy Couture, B.J. Penn, and Conor McGregor, had ever held a championship belt in two different weight divisions. St-Pierre intended to become the fourth.

Georges St-Pierre's thirteen wins in title bouts is tied with Jon Jones for most all-time in UFC history.

Aside from the physical preparation, I was curious how GSP mentally prepares for upcoming fights. "I do a lot of visualization," St-Pierre said. "A lot of scenarios in my head that I repeat and repeat. You try and get in your opponent's mind. Try and study him. Study his behavior and his patterns to see what he is going to try and do to you." These visualizations go incredibly in-depth, as St-Pierre envisions his opponent's strengths and weaknesses, while playing out possible moves he will be forced to counter. At times, he will mentally play out a situation in which he is losing. He would "force myself to think how I'm gonna get out of that bad spot and come back on top. Sometimes, it's human nature to think 'What is the worst thing that can happen?' " St-Pierre said. "We are not always thinking positive. You think about the danger, but it's very important when you do visualizations, you always end in a positive way."

These extensive breakdowns of his opponent tax the fighter's mind. "It drives me completely insane," St-Pierre told me. "It prevents me from sleeping, but that's the price to pay."

When one obsesses over something, they are willing to do whatever it takes. In order to accomplish his goals, St-Pierre put in both the physical and mental work. Later in our conversation, St-Pierre shared with me another motivation tactic he used to prepare for his battles. Ahead of any fight in the UFC, GSP would write his goals for the match. "I would bring this paper [to training camp] and put it on a mirror. For my last fight, I wrote 'On November 4, I will defeat Michael Bisbing and become UFC Middleweight Champion.' Every time I go in front of the mirror to brush my teeth, I see this piece of paper to make me remember why I signed up for this, and why I'm going through the grind."

As you can probably guess, the 1,449-day hiatus from the sport meant nothing to the obsessed, highly calculated star. On November 4, 2017, Georges St-Pierre choked out Michael Bisbing in the third round to become the UFC Middleweight Champion and the fourth fighter in history to obtain two belts in separate weight divisions. He also joined Randy Couture as the only UFC fighters who had three different title reigns. The victory was the twentieth in St-Pierre's UFC career, which tied the record for most all-time.

St-Pierre, who has since announced his retirement for the second time, finished his fighting career with a record of 26–2. The once-poor Canadian who was often bullied in school no longer needs to worry about money or being physically harmed. When asked how rich GSP really is, Dana White, in a 2013 *Forbes* article, said "Georges St-Pierre is our biggest pay-per-view star… He's rich. He's very rich." The article also went on to state that in his title-defending fights against Carlos Condit and Nick Diaz, GSP made around nine million dollars. Keep in mind the millions coming in from sponsors like Under Armour, Hayaboosa, Coca-Cola, NOS and others. Under Armour executive, Steve Battista, told *Forbes* that St-Pierre is the "Michael Jordan of MMA." Remember that two thousand dollars he borrowed for his mother? Yeah, he got around to paying her back and then some.

GSP ended our conversation by stating, "As crazy as I am, I always put my life and the people I love in front of my goals."

So, why is obsessing over a particular hobby or activity so vital? When you're obsessed, you automatically heighten your focus, forcing you to become more present in the moment. The more interest you take in something, the more willing you are to take risks and go out of your comfort zone, especially if it means it will ultimately help you in your field. Despite not knowing English or anything about New York, GSP was willing to step out of his environment and travel to the United States to improve his fighting skills.

When we decide to partake in an activity that we are not necessarily comfortable with, we instinctively broaden our horizons. Doing something out of the ordinary is a prime way to expand our consciousness and help us learn more about who we are and what we are capable of.

Whether we realize it or not, us humans actually exert more positive energy when we spend our days involved in activities that we enjoy. The more positive energy we spread, the happier we will be.

Like developing your passions, an obsession for something will give you that appreciation for failure. Think of something you love to do. Maybe it's a video game or a sport. When you strike out in baseball or get killed by your opponent in *Call of Duty*, you don't quit. You keep going, because you are devoted to that activity.

Obviously, the more fascinated you are by an activity, the more time you are going to put into it. When we put an extended amount of work into one of our hobbies, our chances of being successful increase. We find out what works and what doesn't at a much faster rate since we are willing to dedicate more effort and energy into that specific venture.

Obsession will also compel us to be surrounded by like-minded individuals who share the love for that activity. As we know, a key part of success is who we surround ourselves with, so spending time with those who have similar goals and aspirations will motivate you to be great and work hard.

The beauty of obsession goes way beyond being more goal-oriented and increasing your chances of finding success. When we see progress and growth in our desired field, we will naturally become happier. As humans, personal growth in any facet of life will put a smile on our faces.

Ever wonder why you see so many celebrities and public figures excel in multiple professions? Lebron James is arguably the best basketball player ever but also excelled as an actor. Not only is Drake an incredibly successful music artist, but the Canadian rapper also has his hands in other business ventures. This is possible because they obsessed over their primary field and carried that enthusiasm and work ethic into other activities. Obsession teaches us to not only be great in our desired area, but other domains as well.

Paramount Points

- Find an activity that you enjoy and become *obsessed* with it.

- Becoming obsessed with a particular hobby will speed up your success rate in your desired field.

- The more obsessed you are with something, the more likely it is that you will be surrounded with like-minded individuals who also strive for distinction. This will internally motivate you to focus on self-improvement.

- The more time and energy you put toward your field of choice, the happier you will be.

- If you can't stop thinking about your specific interest, you are on the right path.

CHAPTER FOURTEEN

Don't Ever Stop

"A thatch-roofed house with a dirt floor in the mountains of Southern Bukidnon province at a time where anti-communist militiamen were battling insurgents."

That is how *The Edmonton Journal* described the house and environment that Manny Pacquiao was born into. Sarrangani, where Pacquiao is from, is among one of the poorest regions in the Philippines.

Growing up, the Pacquiao family struggled to get by. There was no money for schooling, and the family rarely had enough cash to purchase a decent meal. One of Manny's uncles, Benito Bequilla, told the *South China Morning Post*, "When they were growing up, Manny and his family used to collect stale bread and heat it up to sell. The family…lived on bananas and root crops. They had no rice most of the time. Manny wore ragged clothes."

Manny's mother, Dionisia Dapidran-Pacquiao, ran a store in the city where she sold bread, doughnuts, and fried peanuts that she had made or gathered. Manny helped his mother out with her business while making a little extra cash for the family. On the side, Manny would collect *calamansi*, lemons native to the Philippines, and sell them on the streets. *Calamansi* is common in the Filipino culture, often used in traditional dishes, beverages, marinades, and preserves.

When Manny was still young, his father, Rosalio Pacquiao, killed the family dog for food. As a sixth grader, Manny and his family found out Rosalio had been living with another woman, and he and Dionisia split. The killing of the family pet and Rosalio's adultery strained Manny and his father's relationship for a handful of years.

At the age of ten, Manny decided to quit school due to his family's severe poverty. Two years later, because of conflict with the militiamen near the family household, the Pacquiaos moved into General Santos City, where Manny's uncle, Sardo Mejia, lived. Pacquiao served as a store assistant for his uncle, collecting sacks of empty bottles of Vino Kulafu, a popular Chinese wine that got its name from an old Filipino comic. Kulafu, originally created in 1933, was a Tarzan-like character. Manny and his brother Bobby, who both lived essentially out of a cardboard box, also sold cigarettes on the street for money.

Luckily for Pacquiao, "Uncle Sardo," as he refers to Mejia, had a passion for fighting. When Mejia introduced Manny to some Betamax videos of heavyweight fights, the young boy was hooked. In his autobiography, Pacquiao explains how his life changed forever after James "Buster" Douglas upset Mike Tyson in 1990. From that point on, Pacquiao decided he would pursue a career in the fight game. "I knew without a doubt I would become a fighter," he said. "I knew that the underdog can, and often does, win."

When I asked Manny of his first childhood memory of fighting, he said, "There was a boxing event every Sunday, and I participated because I learned that there was a cash prize." In the *South China Morning Post*, Mejia recalled when Manny first began to compete as a fighter for a few bucks in front of a tiny crowd on Sundays. "When he started, he had no muscle on him at all and I couldn't see him ever becoming a fighter. Then, after I trained him for six months, I said to myself, 'This boy is going to be a World Champion.' "

"Kid Kulafu," Manny's original boxing name, immediately fell in love with the process of developing as a fighter. When he wasn't out helping the family put food on the table, Pacquiao was training. He would often wake up at four in the morning to go for a run. To show Manny what it took to be great, Mejia rented videotapes of Mike Tyson fights, which the boy studied. He quickly picked up on the professional fighter's tactics and maneuvers.

Soon, Manny Pacquiao started dominating his opponents at the local park in General Santos. One day, a talent scout, looking for young boxers to compete in Manila, noticed Manny's unique skills. Eager to improve and one day become champion, fourteen-year-old Pacquiao got on a boat and headed off to the nation's capital.

In Manila, Pacquiao worked in construction for four dollars an hour, while also training in the mornings and late afternoons. With little money and no family around, Pacquiao would often sleep in the gym he trained at.

When I asked Manny about these hard times, he said, "Experiencing those hardships in life gave me more motivation to work hard and focus on whatever I want to do, especially boxing... My goal was to help my family. My goal was to be [a] champion in the Philippines."

With an impeccable work ethic and incredible drive, Manny quickly caught the eyes of the gym owner, Rod Nazario. Nazario took Pacquiao under his wing and managed and trained him during his teenage years.

In 1995 at the age of sixteen, Manny Pacquiao made his professional debut, which was broadcasted on Vintage Sports' *Blow by Blow*, an evening boxing show. Competing as a light flyweight and weighing in at 106 pounds, Pacquiao defeated Edmund "Enting" Ignacio in unanimous decision. His ultra-aggressive, all-or-nothing kamikaze-style of boxing made

Manny an immediate star. As his body started to develop, Pacquiao moved up to the flyweight division. After twenty-three professional fights, he had a record of 22–1 with 13 KOs. In May 1998, Pacquiao traveled to Japan, where he would knockout Shin Terao in the first round. This victory set Manny up for his first-ever title shot vs. Flyweight Champion, Chatchai Sasakul. The match was set to take place in Thailand, Sasakul's homeland. The Thai boxing star was nearly eight years older than Pacquiao and a heavy favorite. Sasakul turned pro in 1991 and had already defended his title twice.

The day after the fight, if you had checked out the boxing section in *The Home News Tribune*, you would have found that Mike Tyson was set to hold a news conference to announce his return to boxing and his upcoming fight with Francois Botha. If you read all the way to the end of the fighting portion of the newspaper, you would come across the last sentence, "Manny Pacquiao (24–1, 15 KOs) of the Philippines, won the WBC Flyweight title, stopping Thailand's Chatchai Sasakul with a left hook in the eighth round." Although it wasn't what we would call "Headliner News" in the States, Manny Pacquiao was officially a World Champion.

One year later, Pacquiao, who skipped both the super flyweight and bantamweight divisions, defeated Reynante Jamili, earning him the vacant WBC International Super Bantamweight Title. After defending this title five times, knocking out all five opponents, Pacquiao decided it was time to take his talents to the United States.

In 2001, Pacquiao and his team moved to America, eager to find a gym and a trainer who believed in Manny. After meeting with a few trainers, Pacquiao's camp found no success. A handful of coaches had watched him spar, but none were willing to take a chance on Manny, especially since there wasn't much money in Pacquiao's weight-class division. However, a trip to California wound up changing Pacquiao's life.

The man who ended up jumpstarting Pacquiao's career in America was Freddie Roach, a former lightweight boxer. He began his professional career in 1978 and won his first ten bouts. However, after more than fifty professional fights under his belt in 1986, Roach decided to retire from the sport. He stayed connected to the fight game, often hanging out at the gym and dishing out advice to young competitors. Roach, who learned under the great Eddie Futch's (a boxing trainer who worked with Joe Frazier, Ken Norton, Larry Holmes, and Trevor Berbick, four of the five men to defeat Muhammad Ali) tutelage, decided to begin his second career as a trainer.

One day in 2001, a small, 122-pound champion who hailed from the Philippines walked into Roach's Wild Card Gym in Hollywood, California. After just one round of sparring with Pacquiao, Roach knew he had found his guy. Pacquiao had an incredibly powerful left hand, and Roach was certain he could do wonders with the twenty-three-year-old. According to *The Medium*, Roach and Pacquiao instantly "began with heavy mitt practice trying to develop a powerful right hand and more fluid footwork. What immediately struck [Roach] was the intensity with which Pacquiao focused on his instructions and how quickly he caught on." With Roach, Pacquiao's game would become multifaceted. His right hand soon became a devastating weapon, while his footwork drastically improved.

Despite being a champion, Pacquiao was not yet a rich man. When he first began training with Roach, Pacquiao stayed at the Vagabond Inn near Wild Card Gym. At the time, rooms at the flea-infested motel would go for less than fifty dollars a night. When asked about the spot that Pacquiao briefly called home, Roach told the *Tallahassee Democrat*, "The place was crawling with bugs, and it was dirty and disgusting. I couldn't believe he still stayed there." Before it closed down for good, the Florida newspaper tracked down the motel's last sixteen reviews on Yelp: "All gave it the minimum one star, with guest tales including stories of bedbugs, crack pipes found between sheets, dirty clothes left by former guests, and prostitutes milling the corridors." To someone who had lived in gyms and outside in cardboard boxes, this was nothing to Manny. He told *USA Today Sports* in 2015, "That is where I would stay, and it wasn't so bad. I don't need so many things to be happy. It was very close to training."

In June 2001, Manny Pacquiao received his biggest opportunity in his young boxing career. After a competitor was forced to withdraw, Pacquiao jumped in as a late replacement to fight IBF Super Bantamweight title holder Lehlohonolo Ledwaba, at the MGM Grand in Las Vegas. Despite fighting on just two weeks' notice, Pacquiao was ready to go.

Far removed from the days of being mentioned at the tail end of boxing sections in the print media world, the *Los Angeles Times* sports section on June 24, 2001, was headlined "Relentless Challenger Surprises Ledwaba," which was followed by "Boxing: Pacquiao is dominant in winning IBF Super Bantamweight title by TKO."

In the second round of the fight, Pacquiao dropped Ledwaba with a left hook to his head. Four rounds later, a cross to Ledwaba's chin had the fighter struggling to get up. This was then followed by a knock to the jaw, which ended the fight. "I never expected it to be this tough," Ledwaba told the *Los Angeles Times*. "I was waiting to see who my new opponent would be, so I knew nothing about him." This would be the last time an opponent would enter the ring and not know of the five foot five fighter from the Philippines. While he entered the Ledwaba fight somewhat unknown by fans in the States, Pacquiao was here to stay, and, just like Vino Kulafu, got better and better over time.

Over the next decade, Pacquiao went on to completely dominate the sport of boxing in America. He became a three-time *Ring Magazine* and BWAA Fighter of the Year, winning both awards in 2006, 2008, and 2009. The Boxing Writers Association of America (BWAA), WBC, and WBO named Pacquiao the Fighter of the Decade for the 2000s.

In 2011, he received the Best Fighter ESPY Award for the second time in his career. At this point, the Filipino fighter possessed a professional record of 54–3–3. In 2015, according to *Forbes*, Pacquiao was the second highest paid athlete in the world. He went from a room at the Vagabond Inn, to a rented apartment, followed by a nice house near Hancock Park, and now a mansion in Beverly Hills.

When this story was written, Pacquiao had generated almost 20 million dollars in pay-per-view buys and nearly $1.5 billion in revenue for his twenty-four pay-per-view fights. He is the only fighter in history to be named World Champion in eight different weight divisions and has won a total of twelve major world titles.

Like all the greats, Pacquiao has managed to become something bigger than himself. While his personal boxing accolades have done wonders for him and his family, Manny Pacquiao always feels like he can do more to make this world a better place. In 2006, Pacquiao joined the Philippine Army's reserve force as a sergeant. Just like in boxing, he climbed up the ranks quickly, eventually earning the title of Senior Master Sergeant. Pacquiao was also appointed as the Command Sergeant Major of the 15th Ready Reserve Division.

Manny passed the high school equivalency exam in 2007 and has since been awarded a handful of certificates, including an Honorary Degree of Doctor of Humanities (Honoris Causa) by Southwestern University.

In 2009, Pacquiao announced he would run in the 2010 Philippines House of Representatives election at Sarangani, his home region. Although he had lost a 2006 congressional election, Pacquiao avenged his defeat and won the 2010 elections by a landslide. He won again in 2013 and, in 2016, was elected senator. Pacquiao continues to serve as a senator and told me he aims to "Serve honestly and to change the way the government is running right now. Help the people out."

Aside from fighting, politics, and military work, Pacquiao has appeared in a scattering of movies, played in professional basketball leagues, and produced a handful of albums featuring his singing.

"You don't put your fame or accomplishments in your head, or, if you do, you change and become lazy," Pacquiao told me in our conversation. "What I have done, or accomplished, I don't put it in my head. Being humble as a person, that is the key."

When I asked about his versatility, Pacquiao credited his willingness to contribute to so many fields to his desire to compete. "Competing is very good. It's very helpful for us to work hard...develop discipline," he said. "Especially in politics, you have to establish your leadership and [show] how you serve the people."

Despite the immense fame, wealth, and legendary boxing career, Manny Pacquiao remains the same person who grew up dirt poor in the Philippines. When asked about his incredibly successful nephew, Benito Bequilla told the *Post Magazine*, "Manny is just the same as he always was. He has never forgotten us. God has given Manny all the love and the grace. He always cares for his family and his relatives. I think the world of this man. We are all so proud of him."

I decided to take a different approach when talking with Pacquiao and posed the question, "Why do you think God put you on Earth?" While many would assume a professional athlete who is arguably one of the best to ever compete in his field would emphasize his career, Pacquiao's response showed me why he is so respected among his family and gigantic following. "I think the main purpose of Manny Pacquiao in this world is to inspire people. Be an inspiration and an example." Pacquiao noted that personal accomplishments are great, "But the most important thing is the relationships with each other and your faith in God. How you treat each other, how you treat other people. That's the most important thing." The true definition of "The People's Champ."

As a father of five, Pacquiao imprints into his children the same ideas that helped him climb to the top. "Always honor God when you accomplish something," he said. "Big or small. Whatever you have or achieve, always give thanks to the Lord. Stay humble. Do not change."

"So what's next?" I asked. A man this decorated must for sure look to take his foot off the gas at some point and soak in his impact on the world, right?

He said, "I believe that as long as I'm still alive, and God gives me wisdom and knowledge, I can still do more."

Pacquiao wrapped up our discussion by stating, "It doesn't matter if they remember me as a champion or as a boxer, but I want them to remember me as a good person. As an inspiration. The way I treat others. The way I help others."

When it comes to lending an extra hand, Pacquiao lets his actions do all of the talking. Ahead of his box office fight with Floyd Mayweather, Pacquiao purchased nine hundred tickets for his family and friends. Keep in mind, the worst seat in the house that night at the Grand Garden Arena in Las Vegas was $1,500.

According to the Manny Pacquiao Foundation, Pacquiao has grossed over half a billion dollars through boxing and endorsements and has donated an estimated one-third of his career earnings to charity. Back in the Philippines, Pacquiao has initiated a variety of public service projects, including the construction of 1,500 homes on the island of Mindanao. Pacquiao also assisted fishermen by purchasing an armada of new boats for the anglers.

Kulafu, the previously referenced comic book hero, wore clothes made from the skin of a tiger, making the story unrealistic since there are no tigers in the Philippines. But if I told you a kid, who grew up dirt poor and spent countless nights sleeping at public gyms, would go on to become a senator in his home country, donate over $300 million to charities and public service ventures, and be recognized as one of the greatest fighters in boxing history, you would probably think that's also far-fetched.

Remember the *calamansi* lemons Pacquiao used to collect and sell in order for his family to eat? The native lemon that can be used in sauces, stews, juices, and a smattering of other dishes?

I think it's safe to say that the fruit's well-rounded traits may have rubbed off on the "Pac-Man."

Manny Pacquiao is the only eight-division World Champion in the history of boxing.

No matter what you accomplish in life, you can always do more. When you find success in your field of choice, help the next one up. There is always room for improvement and always someone else you can assist and inspire. Set goals, work hard to achieve them, and then set bigger ones.

What separates the greats from average individuals are their mindsets. In order to live a life of true happiness and fulfillment, we must be bigger than ourselves. Our purpose must go beyond personal accolades and success. Choose to inspire a generation through your actions. Choose to help others with your knowledge.

In 2008, Michael Norton, assistant professor at the Harvard Business School, coordinated a string of studies that revolved around citizens and their income. Norton, along with his colleagues Elizabeth Dunn and Lara Aknin, gathered 632 Americans and asked each individual about their level of income and how their earnings were spent. These questions were followed up with an inquiry on how they would rate their personal happiness. Following the evaluation, Norton and company concluded that those who spent money on others rather than themselves reported to be happier than those who were more selfish with their money.

Research done at the London School of Economics reported that the more volunteer work an individual takes part in, the happier that individual becomes. Not only has an unselfish lifestyle been shown to lower blood pressure and stress levels, but according to research done at the University of Buffalo, people who give and perform selfless acts could be adding years to their lives.

The one constant I learned from speaking to these super-athletes is that there is truly no "I made it" feeling. These men and women are *never satisfied*. You must adopt the "All gas, no brakes" lifestyle. By keeping your foot on the pedal, you are forcing yourself to always move forward. The moment you take your foot off the accelerator, just know that someone out there is getting ready to pass you.

Paramount Points

- You can always do more. Never stop inspiring.
- *Be humble.*
- When you find success, just know that there are thousands of others working to take your spot. Don't let up!
- Never forget where you came from.
- Enjoy every step of the way on your path to glory.
- Helping others leads to more happiness.

The Last Time I Saw Dr. Seuss

"Dr. Seuss I did it! I accomplished my feat!
Trust the Grind is finally complete!"

"You wrote a book, your dream has come true,
But Jeremy, there is plenty more to do.
Accomplishing this goal should feel great,
But let's set more to attain at a later date.

You see, as long as we are still breathing,
There is always something else we can be achieving.
I know you put in a lot of work to finalize this project,
So take a moment to acknowledge the kind words and respect.

As you get ready to set bigger goals,
Let me give you some advice that you can pass to other souls:
Always work toward something.
Possess confidence as if you're a king.

Continue to read, and never stop learning!
That way, your mind will always be churning.
Be a good listener around your peers.
When someone else talks, be all ears.

When you wake up, express gratitude.
Enter every situation with the proper attitude.
Anything is possible with the right mindset,
So go out and try, don't ever regret.

Always spread love to family and friends.
No matter what, look at life through a positive lens.
Focus on personal progress.
Avoid feeling any sort of stress!

Paige VanZant said to never compare yourself to the rest.
Ms. Kastor reminded us to always believe that you're the best.
Adopt particular habits from successful stars,
But don't get frustrated if you don't own six cars!

We all walk in different shoes
And have unique sets of views.
State your goals out loud like Chipper Jones,
Stay driven like the great Terrell Owens.

Jason Kidd wrote in a journal to stay disciplined,
So do that, and develop your passions like Sheckler did.
Ryan Lochte made sacrifices to win that gold.
Gary Player works out every day! Even as he gets old!

Mike Modano set aside time to mentally lock in,
GSP obsessed over his profession and did whatever it took to win.
At a young age, Andruw Jones told himself that he would be great.
Devin Hester didn't let his unfavorable circumstances
control his fate.

Luis Gonzalez wasn't afraid to fail,
Tim Hudson showed if you believe in yourself, you'll prevail!
Make sure to identify your "why" like Jimmie Johnson.

Be like Pac-man, and aim to inspire an entire generation.
Follow my advice, and happiness is what you will find.
Stay humble, and always remember to Trust the Grind."

Conclusion

Let's Go

All the athletes in this story were just like you. You might be familiar with Powerade's "Just a Kid" campaign for the 2016 Olympics, but seriously, we are all just a kid from somewhere! While we don't get to choose where we start out or who brings us into this world, we all have a choice each and every day we wake up: either get better or get worse. After reading these stories, you have now absorbed all the information you need to become successful.

So set goals. Say them out loud. Write them down. In fact, scribble down, not only aspirations, but thoughts, feelings, and anything else that comes to mind. Develop discipline in whatever field you choose to spend your time in. No matter what the outcome, stay driven and obsessed in that field.

Do your mind and body a favor and fuel up with the right foods. Stick to coffee, water, and tea. Get a workout in whenever you can. Develop a routine in both the kitchen and the gym.

When you enter a high-pressure situation, be confident. Remember, confidence is a decision. Don't run away from failure. The mishaps and hardships in life strengthen our mind.

When you are in pursuit of greatness, make sacrifices. As you know, you'll be happier in the long run when you see that hard work truly pays off.

When times get tough, remain positive. Recall your purpose and why you do what you do.

Most importantly, be yourself. The more you stay true to yourself, the happier you will be. Don't try to be someone you're not. Who cares what the person next to you is doing? They aren't you and don't possess the gifts that you have.

When you make it, *keep grinding*. Help others whenever you get the chance. Smile, spread love, and you'll always rise above.

Jeremy

Let's Connect

Twitter/Instagram: @JeremyTheGrind

With the hashtag #TrustTheGrind, send me:

- A picture of the healthy foods you're eating

- Your goals

- Your experiences of going out of your comfort zone

- An example of how you overcame adversity

- An example of a failure you overcame with hard work to achieve success

- Sacrifices you are making while you accomplish a certain feat

- Someone/something in your life you are thankful for

- A fire verse that you either wrote or heard from another artist

About the Author

Jeremy Bhandari was born in Ashland, Massachusetts, on June 19, 1996. Unlike the plurality of babies born in the twentieth century, Jeremy wriggled into the world in his mother's bedroom, rather than a hospital. His rare arrival on Earth is ironically symbolic with his life story.

Before dropping him off at preschool, Jeremy's mother would spread out the sports section in the *Boston Globe* for her son to examine while he ate his breakfast. Jeremy, at just four-years-old, would study the MLB standings and league leaders. At this point, circa 2001, all the Massachusetts baseball fanatics obsessed over Pedro Martinez and Nomar Garciaparra, two stars on the Boston Red Sox. When it was time for Jeremy to select his favorite player for the back of his Tee Ball card, the calculated cherub demanded that Alex Rodriguez, a shortstop for the Texas Rangers, be labeled on his individualized square. While Jeremy probably couldn't locate Texas on a map, he knew that Rodriguez was leading the American League in home runs, so why not classify him as his front-runner?

Jeremy's love for sports continued to maturate as he grew older. In elementary school, he started writing fictionalized stories of baseball games, where one team would always make an epic comeback in the late-innings. Fast forward to his junior year at UMass Amherst, and Jeremy was still scripting about sports. After handing in a paper on the relationship between spending and winning in the MLB, Jeremy decided to take writing more seriously. At 23-years-old, Jeremy signed a contract with Mango Publishing and wrote *Trust The Grind*.

Aside from writing, Jeremy puts a strong emphasis on physical fitness, and spreading love to all those around him

Mango Publishing, established in 2014, publishes an eclectic list of books by diverse authors—both new and established voices—on topics ranging from business, personal growth, women's empowerment, LGBTQ studies, health, and spirituality to history, popular culture, time management, decluttering, lifestyle, mental wellness, aging, and sustainable living. We were recently named 2019's #1 fastest growing independent publisher by *Publishers Weekly*. Our success is driven by our main goal, which is to publish high-quality books that will entertain readers as well as make a positive difference in their lives.

Our readers are our most important resource; we value your input, suggestions, and ideas. We'd love to hear from you—after all, we are publishing books for you!

Please stay in touch with us and follow us at:

Facebook: Mango Publishing
Twitter: @MangoPublishing
Instagram: @MangoPublishing
LinkedIn: Mango Publishing
Pinterest: Mango Publishing

Sign up for our newsletter at www.mangopublishinggroup.com and receive a free book!

Join us on Mango's journey to reinvent publishing, one book at a time.